R. S. THOMAS

W. MOELWYN MERCHANT

THE UNIVERSITY OF ARKANSAS PRESS

Fayetteville   London   1990

94 93 92 91 90 5 4 3 2 1

Typeface: Goudy Old Style

The paper used in this publication meets the minimum requirements of the American National Standard for Permanence of Paper for Printed Library Materials Z39.48-1984. ∞

LIBRARY OF CONGRESS CATALOGING-IN-PUBLICATION DATA

Merchant, W. Moelwyn (William Moelwyn), 1913–
    R.S. Thomas / W. Moelwyn Merchant.
        p. cm.
    Reprint. Originally published: [Cardiff] : University of Wales
Press on behalf of the Welsh Arts Council, 1979. Originally
published in series: Writers of Wales.
    Includes bibliographical references.
    ISBN 1-55728-162-9 (alk. paper).
    1. Thomas, R. S. (Ronald Stuart), 1913–   —Criticism and
interpretation.   I. Title.   II. Title: RS Thomas.
PR6039.H618Z76   1990
821'.914—dc20   89-49708
                                                              CIP

Preface

It is a great personal pleasure that this brief study of the remarkable poet R. S. Thomas is reissued. The study was originally commissioned by the Welsh Arts Council and published in limited edition in the Writers of Wales series in 1979. Though so many honours have been granted to R. S. Thomas, it is perhaps only in the next years that his full stature will be realized. I have written elsewhere that R. S. Thomas is for me one of the three great landmarks in the poetry of Wales : Dafydd ap Gwilym, Henry Vaughan and Thomas himself. I was led to that judgement by the spare discipline of his verse and the long spiritual journey which that verse chronicled.

It seemed to me that that long spiritual exploration came to its climax in the volume *Frequencies* (1978) — and that is the reason why I have not felt impelled to extend this book, to consider the volumes that have appeared since it was written. The poems now have attained a new tranquillity, though the search is at least as strenuous as before. Where Henry Vaughan 'saw Eternity the other night', so R. S. Thomas was content to 'stare

over into the eternal
silence that is the repose of God.'

He must also be content now to be poised 'somewhere between faith and doubt' and to explore the mystic's language of negatives in which

'Godhead
is the colonisation by mind
of untenanted space.'

It is a vast and solemn quest and R.S. Thomas, whether he is pursuing truth in the concerns of Wales or searching for Godhead in the spaces between the stars, has never flinched from the consequences, in thought or action.

Moelwyn Merchant

I

A poet is under no obligation to create a consistent 'world-view' nor has he any commitment to his reader to commend a 'philosophy'. He writes with integrity as his successive needs, impulses, ideas, images press upon him; the unity and consistency of his work will spring solely from its growing revelation of a many-faceted personality.

The writings of R. S. Thomas in poetry and prose have been prolific and span over thirty years of publication. They have appeared to many readers and critics to have a direct, even disarming simplicity and to compass a very limited and readily available range of themes, and this judgement has considerably obscured much of the profundity, the ambiguity and even the contradictions in his work. Nor are these contradictions entirely thematic and ideal; equally disconcerting are the complex and sharp changes of tone within the same poem, contradictions which sharply modify the comfortable picture of a parson-poet arranging his simple and austere melodies for a very limited range of instruments. A close examination of these ambivalences in his work substantially increases the stature of this passionately single-minded but complex writer and it is the purpose of this essay to develop a critical portrait with all its thorny contradictions.

R. S. Thomas has been very sparing in the autobiographical hints he has placed in the poetry but those who read Welsh will find a most moving account of his early days in the broadcast, Y Llwybrau Gynt (1972). For the greater part of his life, the significant events for us are the movements of his priestly ministry in the Church in Wales and the dates of his publications. It is nonetheless valuable to begin where he does, in the opening paragraph of the broadcast:

> Tua diwedd y Rhyfel Byd Cyntaf yw hi, a'r lle: Penrhyn Wirral, Sir Gaer. Y mae bachgen bach yn chwarae ar y traeth. Dros y môr tua'r

1

de-orllewin y mae bryniau uchel, llwydlas i'w gweld. Cyfeiria ei dad atynt. 'That's Wales', medde fe. Mae'r bachgen yn codi ei ben am eiliad a syllu arnynt, cyn troi'n ôl i chwarae efo'r tywod. Myfi yw'r bachgen hwn ar fy ngwyliau efo'm rhieni o Lerpwl.

(The time: near the end of the First World War, and the place: the Wirral Peninsula, Cheshire. A little boy is playing on the beach. Across the sea to the south-west, high, grey-blue hills can be seen. His father points to them. 'That's Wales', he says. The boy lifts his head for a moment and gazes at them, then turns to his playing in the sand. I am that boy, on holiday from Liverpool with my parents.)

— a moment full of minute tensions which, man-size, were to be present through the years.

Ronald Stuart Thomas was born in Cardiff in 1913 and graduated in the University of Wales, reading Classics in the University College of North Wales, Bangor. He was ordained in the Church in Wales in 1937 and in 1942 went to his first country living as rector of the parish of Manafon in Montgomeryshire, where his sermons and ministry are still remembered with affectionate awe. This gentle and fertile countryside, with its upland sheepruns, near the meeting-point of rural Wales with a rural Englishry, was to become the nursing-ground for twelve years of the major themes of his work; the three volumes, *The Stones of the Field* (1946), *An Acre of Land* (1952) and *The Minister* (1953) set the main lines of his creativity for the succeeding twenty years. In 1954 he became vicar of another small country parish, St Michael's, Eglwys Fach in north Dyfed, a few miles south of Machynlleth and this living was to see the establishment of his wide reputation, with his receiving the Heinemann Award of the Royal Society of Literature in 1959 and the Queen's Gold Medal for Poetry in 1964. During these years the major volumes of his maturity were published: *Song at the Year's Turning* (1955), which gathered up the central work of the three earlier volumes and extended their lines with a collection of nineteen new poems; *Poetry for Supper* (1958), *Tares* (1961), *The Bread of Truth* (1963) and *Pietà* (1966) completed the rich material that came out of his time at Eglwys Fach. In the next year, in 1967, he moved into the diocese of Bangor, becoming vicar of Eglwys Hywyn Sant at Aberdaron on the tip of the Llŷn Peninsula; there, in 1968, he received the Welsh Arts Council major Prize of Honour for his contribution to the literature of Wales

2

and for the next ten years his publications increased in intensity: *Not That He Brought Flowers* (1968), *H'm* (1972), *Young and Old* (1972, in the series of Chatto Poets for the Young), *What is a Welshman?* (1974, published by Christopher Davies), *Laboratories of the Spirit* (1975), *The Way of It* (1977, published with drawings by Barry Hirst, at the Ceolfrith Press, in Sunderland Arts Centre), and, his final volume before retiring from the parochial ministry in the same year, *Frequencies* (1978). *Selected Poems* appeared in 1973 and to this very substantial publication of poetry, both at Eglwys Fach and during the prolific decade at Aberdaron, must be added much important work in four complementary fields: his comparatively rare contributions in prose, more especially to the journal *Wales*; his significant editing of anthologies, the brief introductions to which reveal a great deal of his presiding ideas and austerely discriminating taste: *The Batsford Book of Country Verse* (1961), *The Penguin Book of Religious Verse* (1962, his most important and revealing anthology), *Selected Poems of Edward Thomas* (1964) and, very appositely, *A Choice of George Herbert's Verse* (1967) and *A Choice of Wordsworth's Verse* (1971). Two other single works complete the picture: the publication in the United States of *The Mountains* (1968), his most engaging piece of English prose, admirably complementary to the austere wood-engravings of Reynolds Stone after drawings in Snowdonia by John Piper — a centrally significant work, despite its relative brevity and its critical neglect; and *Abercuawg*, his brilliantly imaginative Welsh address at the Royal National Eisteddfod at Cardigan in 1976 (Gwasg Gomer, 1976), focusing with poetic clarity and in a very flexible prose the nature of his Welshness and his personal aspirations for his country. Just as his poetry takes on a new dimension when it is heard in his public readings (he is one of the two or three finest readers of poetry today), so his prose works are a necessary supplement to our understanding of his verse; they provide not so much a corrective to the argument of ideas conducted in his volumes of poetry as a delicate reorientation of those ideas and an adjustment of their tone. Indeed they sometimes reveal a tone of romanticism that is almost entirely absent from the verse.

II

In the Poetry Book Society *Bulletin* for Christmas 1968, R. S. Thomas declared without diffidence, 'I play on a small pipe, a little aside from the main road.' That self-judgement coincided with the publication of *Not That He Brought Flowers*, until then his most far-ranging collection, compassing moments in contemporary Welsh affairs (the anger of Tryweryn in 'Reservoirs'), his most mature comments on the pastoral ministry ('The Priest'), moments of response to the Spanish landscape and to painters and painting. Yet the judgement remained in a certain sense valid. To return to the beginning: the selection from *An Acre of Land* in *Song at the Year's Turning* closes with two related poems, 'The One Furrow' and 'Farm Child'. In the former, having defined the intellectual, exploratory young man 'in the mind's pride', he asks,

> Then who is it taught me back to go
> To cattle and barrow,
> Field and plough;
> To keep to the one furrow,
> As I do now?

Part of the answer lies validly in the next poem, the fascination of the Farm Child's 'unconscious grace'; this 'poise' is both gracious and graceful and in each poem the apparent limitation of aim, the deliberately narrowed focus of vocation, is concerned with the absolutely essential, the basic activity which preserves life: in 'The One Furrow' the objects of activity are

> cattle and barrow,
> Field and plough;

in 'Farm Child' the end is still more explicit:

4

Notice his poise, from such conscious grace
Earth breeds and beckons to the stubborn plough.

The collaboration with earth's fecundity is the basic theme from the beginning of his work. The second poem in *The Stones of the Field*, 'A Labourer', is poised between the apparent reduction of identity through toil — 'his face is smooth, inscrutable as stone' — and the sharply unexpected character of earth — 'the sweet pregnancy that yields his bread'.

This is the context of the most arresting poem to confront the reader in the first collection, 'A Peasant', Iago Prytherch's first entrance. From his neutral introduction as 'just an ordinary man of the bald Welsh hills', the language becomes a calculated affront, dismissing the repellent worker, with his 'half-witted grin of satisfaction, his spittled mirth' and his crude fatigue, 'Motionless, except when he leans to gob in the fire', to be finally rejected by the judgement:

There is something frightening in the vacancy of his mind.

But it is at this point that the poem turns upon itself in full ambiguity:

His clothes, sour with years of sweat
And animal contact, shock the refined,
But affected, sense with their stark naturalness.

That poised turn at the end of the line, 'the refined,/but affected, sense', redirects the critical emotion upon the observer and away from the peasant; with this release the peasant himself becomes the potential subject of a minute epic:

Yet this is your prototype, who, season by season
Against siege of rain and the wind's attrition,
Preserves his stock, an impregnable fortress
Not to be stormed even in death's confusion.
Remember him, then, for he, too, is a winner of wars,
Enduring like a tree under the curious stars.

The critic's fastidious refinement, seen here as affectation, cannot compass 'stark naturalness', cannot therefore compass that universal element in the peasant's relation to the earth which gives each unique

5

Iago Prytherch his significance; in this perspective, the sweat and the spittle are almost irrelevant, the unavoidable but unimportant by-products of the struggle with earth and the elements.

This careful discrimination informs the very early poem in the collection, 'Out of the Hills'. We follow the journey of the shepherd out of his 'starved pastures' to the village where he can drink and where

> his scaly eye
> Sloughs its cold care and glitters. The day is his
> To dabble a finger in.

His drunkenness is a 'sudden disintegration of his soul's hardness', the two words 'disintegration' and 'hardness' held in a balanced apposition of appraisal, neutralizing their criticism of the peasant's nature, which, we are reminded, is a product of the 'traditional discipline of flint and frost'. When the shepherd returns drunk at midnight, 'the earth is patient; he is not lost', the closing word carrying a delicate ambiguity — he neither strays nor is damned. And if the earth is harsh with flint, clod, frost and wind, there is also the 'medicinal sun' and 'the summer's sweetness'.

Throughout these early poems — and it is a tone that Thomas has preserved through four decades of published poetry — facts repellent and attractive are chronicled with clarity and there is no flicker of deviation into patronage, censoriousness or pity.

There are, then, no simple antitheses in these poems. They would have great dramatic interest if such an antithesis — the instinctive pastoral compassion of the priest confronting an object of apparent disgust — were their mainspring. But there is in fact neither antithesis nor reconciliation of attitude; both reactions, of compassionate admiration and distaste, are held, irreconcilable, within the texture of the poem and if an attitude is to be defined here at all, it is of total acceptance, recording grace and shame within these lives, with understanding, neutral charity and compassion.

A later poem in the collection 'Affinity' carries the argument, from its title onward, a good deal more piquantly forward. The poem opens with apparently neutral detachment and from a height:

> Consider this man in the field beneath.

A sensitive affinity with this 'vague somnambulist' is not easy as he pursues his apparently vacant life,

Stumbling insensitively from furrow to furrow.

The poet however questions the validity of his own easy assumptions concerning peasant gracelessness:

From the standpoint of education or caste or creed
Is there anything to show that your essential need
Is less than his?

This deft irony which puts the sophisticate at the disadvantage appears to be modulated in later lines; indeed, were the poem to end with a virtual repetition of the repellent qualities with which other poems in the collection make us familiar —

Don't be taken in
By stinking garments or an aimless grin;
He also is human —

we should be left with an ironic understatement, patronizing to the point of unseemliness; the irony is in fact there but given yet another turn, to compassion in the closing phrases:

He also is human, and the same small star,
That lights you homeward, has inflamed his mind
With the old hunger, born of his kind.

Here then is the 'affinity' of the title but the tight organization of the poem allows a further degree of irony. In the calculus of qualities established in the comparison between peasant and observer the balance is poised disconcertingly on the matter of duty and obligation. If the peasant's life is impoverished and superficially repellent, what has the sophisticated intelligence to offer?

Ransack your brainbox, pull out the drawers
That rot in your head's dust, and what have you to give
To enrich his spirit or the way he lives?

In this poem, as in so many others, R. S. Thomas appears to establish a tone of detachment, of almost clinical observation, to deny it by

7

both irony and a sudden shock of invective. It is a complexity both of tone and poetic organization which marks these early poems with outstanding maturity.

Despite the generalizations concerning the peasant's 'kind', he is never, for Thomas, an abstraction, a class of men. Indeed, in these early poems he devotes fewer lines to the large, fundamental themes, the land's tending or the movement of the seasons, than to the slight but revealing detail: the raised hand of 'Peasant's Greeting' with its disturbingly ambiguous message:

> The land's patience and a tree's
> Knotted endurance and
> The heart's doubt whether to curse or bless,
> All packed into a single gesture,

or the returning labourer's anger in 'Ire' at finding

> the table unlaid and bare
> As a boar's backside.

One cannot leave this first volume without placing two poems in apposition, 'A Priest to his People', the central poem in the collection, and the neglected 'The Airy Tomb', not subsequently reprinted after *Song at the Year's Turning*. 'A Priest to his People' is harshly concise in placing the dilemmas of a country parson. Through all the volumes of verse he has subsequently published, R. S. Thomas has exercised great reserve in theological and pastoral statement, allowing a credal or priestly standpoint to emerge from the rare phrase or image embedded in the seemingly objective verse. But this poem is explicit even in its contradictory stances. The opening lines are violent, sharper in tone than any other poem in the collection:

> Men of the hills, wantoners, men of Wales,
> With your sheep and your pigs and your ponies, your
>   sweaty females,
> How I have hated you for your irreverence, your scorn even
> Of the refinements of art and the mysteries of the Church.

His sermons, by which he would mediate his ideas, his subtle union of art and theology, are momentarily revealed in their tragic ineffectiveness:

8

I whose invective would spurt like a flame of fire
To be quenched always in the coldness of your stare.

The men and women before him in the pews, shaped, carved to their
present state by unremitting labour, are recognized as

Men of bone wrenched from the bitter moorland,
Who have not yet shaken the moss from your savage
skulls,
Or prayed the peat from your eyes.

The confrontation appears final, with no resolution in emotion,
whether of anger or admiration, nor even the neutrality of tolerance.
What the priest has to minister is a long tradition in which art
mediates the 'mysteries of the Church' (not theology, the inert ground
plan, but the living truth) to which the peasant, 'curt and graceless',
has no instrument of response. Yet the priest in the poet acquiesces
in the pagan substratum of the peasant's strength:

And all the devices of church and school
Have failed to cripple your unhallowed movements,
Or put a halter on your wild soul...
And why should you come like sparrows for prayer-crumbs,
Whose hands can dabble in the world's blood.

The reprehension of the peasant's ways and superficial appearance
is not therefore a rejection of his paganism or earthiness; R. S. Thomas
shares these and indeed he once remarked to me that his most vivid
response to the peninsula of Llŷn was not to the Christian remains
but to the archaeology, the geology behind them. This points the
essential difference between him and his peasant subject, that the
poet can articulate the primitive relationship between the two
experiences, pagan and Christian.

This would appear to lead in the poem to the acceptance of an
impasse, the priest's complex conviction negated by the peasant's
rejection of 'all that I can offer', and his indifference to the Church's
'praise or blame'. But the poem denies the impasse and ends
courteously with a recognition of the two ways, the peasant's and
the priest's — 'you will continue to unwind your days'. And yet we
are denied a conclusion in mere courteous acceptance of differing
modes of life. In the last analysis it is the priest-poet who is confronted

9

with judgement and the final dilemma; for the permanence of the countryman's way of life remains — and with this the poem ends —

> To affront, bewilder, yet compel my gaze.

This poem is unusually analytic and in its scrupulous and unsentimental integrity, establishes the tone of the few but significant poems concerning the priestly ministry in his later work. 'The Airy Tomb' is a longer, more loose-limbed poem, providing a more meditative look at the one side of the equation, the life of the solitary peasant. It is all there in the schoolboy:

> Books and sums were poison to Tomos, he was stone blind
> To the printer's magic; yet his grass-green eye
> Missed neither swoop nor swerve of the hawk's wing.

After his father's death Twm became 'heir to the lean patch of land' and there follows a strange passage concerning his father's grave:

> But his heart was hurt
> By the gash in the ground, and too few, too few,
> Were the tears that he dropped for the lonely man
> Beginning his journey to annihilation;

a journey that for bird and beast involved

> A wide sepulchre of quiet, blue air

but for the man,

> The board's strictness, and an ugly scar
> On the earth's surface.

The tale then becomes Wordsworthian in its compass and manner, a tragic history of growing dereliction. Certain scars of mind and 'prim churchyard' were healed but the widow's bitter isolation, to which 'Twm was bumpkin blind', ends in early death, with Tomos finally alone in 'that grim house, nailed to the mountain side'. There is no change, no incident, no concrete tragedy, save Twm's fate,

> That wound solitary as a brook through the crimson heather,
> Trodden only by sheep, where youth and age
> Met in the circle of a buzzard's flight.

Before the poem ends we are back with the characteristic poised judgement of R.S. Thomas's poems of peasant life. Thus far the poem has seemed a record of rustic insensitivity, a denial both of the mind and the heart's pieties. But the poem ends differently, with lighter brush-strokes which soften the picture:

> and a fortnight gone
> Was the shy soul from the festering flesh and bone
> When they found him there, entombed in the lucid weather.

The 'Airy Tomb' of the title then carries an unusual weight of significance, of the stifling peasant way of life, of the scarring of man's disintegration but, in the last analysis, a refuge for the countryman's 'shy soul' not in the bruit of the elements but in 'lucid weather'. Whether he be Tomos or Iago, though aspects of his life affront our senses, he remains to compel our unexpected attention and compassion.

In this exploration of the first part of the peasant/priest equation, R.S. Thomas has allowed himself unwonted space to work in, some one hundred and fifty-five lines, about ten times his normal span. For all its self-consciousness concerning its mode (its appeal to the 'hypocrite reader', to our weariness with this 'odd tale' and our assumed need for 'the usual climax' in a romantic resolution), this is an especially successful poem, leaving us with the regret that Thomas has not oftener allowed himself this space in which to develop the ambiguities of his subject.

The second half of the equation, the working out of the complexities of the priestly life, is occasionally focused in his reverence for the church building itself. 'Country Church (Manafon)' was of course the place of his ministry during the writing of The Stones of the Field and it is realized as a stone chalice or font, the sacramental centre of a priest's life:

> The church stands, built from the river stone,
> Brittle with light, as though a breath could shatter
> Its slender frame, or spill the limpid water,
> Quiet as sunlight, cupped within the bone.

The tone of this conceit, admirable in its repose, provides the precise counterpoise to the confession in 'A Priest to his People' of his

11

initial hatred,
My first intolerance of your uncouth ways,

and many years later in *Song at the Year's Turning* (1955) this poem out of Manafon comes to its fruition in an equally brief poem, 'In a Country Church', which is one of the finest. Here the coolness of the stone chalice has crystallized still further to the condition 'of the grave saints, rigid in glass'; as the priest kneels in the empty church there is only 'the wind's song' and the 'dry whisper of unseen wings / Bats not angels'. Yet this stone vessel is now more than font or chalice, a place of spirituality transcending the customary sacramental instruments:

> Was he balked by silence? He kneeled long,
> And saw love in a dark crown
> Of thorns blazing, and a winter tree
> Golden with fruit of a man's body.

But this was in the future, a poem from a later maturity. The art of this first volume of 1946, so indicative of the complexity that was to come, was content to be confined within its narrow plot of ground. And already we feel the cutting edge, the words finely honed.

III

An Acre of Land, first published in 1952, stratifies its emotions and themes to a degree that appears to impair its unity; yet the volume in no way conveys a tone of compromise. The poem 'Memories' has a new mildness ('I will sing the land's praises') and Iago Prytherch is made the instrument of apparent reconciliation:

> Come, Iago my friend, and let us stand together
> Now in the time of the mild weather,

this new-found companionship making possible a new function for poetry, to mediate for the silent countryman,

> making articulate
> Your strong feelings, your thoughts of no date,
> Your secret learning, innocent of books.

Iago is no longer 'surly', a rejecter of life's grace; he is simply inarticulate, his lips 'sealed by a natural reticence'. Yet his eyes can speak for him and betray

> The heart's rich harvest, gathered seasons ago.

This idyllic pastoral portrait is confirmed and extended in the tenderest poem in the collection, 'The Evacuee', where not simply the natural order but the whole country community lays its healing power on the child waiting fearfully for the warning of air-raids:

> And so she grew, a small bird in the nest
> Of welcome that was built about her,
> Home now after so long away
> In the flowerless streets of the drab town.

13

And this is no temporary respite but a full assimilation into the new life:

> The men watched her busy with the hens,
> The soft flesh ripening warm as corn.

The community itself is conscious of its gift and in its compassion expands into awareness of a new emotion, a new validity in their natural existence:

> The men watched her, and, nodding, smiled
> With earth's charity, patient and strong.

This is the gentler tone (insufficiently noticed in the poetry of R. S. Thomas) which validates his vision of Wales in the old mythology (as distinct from the historical scars of war and oppression):

> The owl, the ousel, and the toad's carousal
> In Cors Fochno of the old laws.

With a slight shift this unobtrusive wit can accommodate a new view of the farm hand, 'Cynddylan on a Tractor':

> Gone the old look that yoked him to the soil;
> He's a new man now, part of the machine,
> His nerves of metal and his blood oil,

a more kindly irony than the earlier volume would have led us to expect. Yet, astringently alongside these poems, we hear the earlier tones intensified and with a more explicit gloss on the facts recorded. 'The Welsh Hill Country' shatters the pastoral idyll with its clear sight of

> The fluke and the foot-rot and the fat maggot
> Gnawing the skin from the small bones

while the houses silt into the dead land,

> The moss and the mould on the cold chimneys,
> The nettles growing through the cracked doors.

In place of a beneficent order welcoming home the evacuee, or even a literary stereotype 'arranged romantically in the usual manner', we

14

are now confronted with the reality of the farmer of Ty'n-y-Fawnog, a phthisic labourer,

> Contributing grimly to the accepted pattern.

There is moreover a new rhetoric in 'The Hill Farmer Speaks', in which the tyranny of the land is deplored, and its dehumanizing quality recognized:

> I am the farmer, stripped of love
> And thought and grace by the land's hardness;
> But what I am saying over the fields'
> Desolate acres, rough with dew,
> Is, Listen, listen, I am a man like you.

This rhetoric would perhaps be unacceptable but for the latent suggestion in a companion poem, 'Death of a Peasant', of the priest's helplessness in face of dire poverty and loneliness:

> You remember Davies? He died, you know,
> With his face to the wall, as the manner is
> Of the poor peasant in his stone croft
> On the Welsh hills.

Yet through all the smothered compassion, Thomas's voice is frequently raised in a more explicit rejection than that of 'A Priest to his People' in the first volume. 'Valediction' makes no concession:

> You failed me, farmer . . .
> The two things
> That could redeem your ignorance, the beauty
> And grace that trees and flowers labour to teach,
> Were never yours, you shut your heart against them,

and the poem ends in a rejection more final than any heard in *Stones of the Field*:

> For this I leave you
> Alone in your harsh acres.

R. S. Thomas comments rarely on the form or the stuff of his poetry but a grave remark in a private conversation throws much light on the severity of this poem by contrast with the small moments of mitigating compassion in the earlier poems: 'When a farm labourer is docking mangels he has little time for art and I don't blame his indifference — but if he loses his "moral" nature, then he's truly lost.' It is a distinction which makes its point at so many stages in his work.

It is at this moment that we first meet 'the matter of Wales' fully articulated in R. S. Thomas's work. 'The Rising of Glyndŵr' in *The Stones of the Field*, distanced in its ballad form, had not prepared us for the new astringency in the second volume. The violence of Glyndŵr's bid for power is there, the menace is named, but is scarcely felt behind the literary tone and its archaisms:

> Then he spoke, and anger kindled
> In each brooding eye;
> Swords and spears accused the sky,
> The woods resounded with a bitter cry.

The transition to a new tone is made delicately in *An Acre of Land*. The titles of the volumes themselves have shifted from the biblical compact of Job with the stones of the field (a universal, non-specific relation between man and the natural order) to Siôn Tudur's more precise, 'domestic' insight that man has no security without his relation to the soil, his 'acre of land':

> Nid câr da ond acer o dir.

Literary melancholy still sounds in the new volume, in words that have the allusive sadness of old unhappy things, as in the poem 'Wales':

> I hear the ousel of Cilgwri telling
> The mournful story of the long dead.

The relatively long poem, 'The Tree: Owain Glyndŵr Speaks', darkens the mood but the brooding is still meditative, intellectually distanced:

> I heard
> Above the tuneful consonants
> The sharp anguish, the despair
> Of men beyond my smooth domain
> Fretting under the barbed sting
> Of English law.

16

The vision of the future is muted and we hear most clearly not the sounds of rebellion in the 'new spring' but the romantic nostalgia of the lost glory:

> the long nights
> Of wine and music on the hearth
> Of Sycharth of the open gates.

But the two companion poems, 'Welsh History' and 'Welsh Landscape', establish the darker tone. The first of these catalogues the old losses:

> We were a people taut for war...
> Our kings died, or they were slain
> By the old treachery at the ford...
> We were a people bred on legends...
> We were a people wasting ourselves
> In fruitless battles for our masters...

and all this tautens until it expresses fully the significant 'leitmotiv':

> We were a people and are so yet.

This is no dramatic stance, a public patriotic gesture of little significance; it is the fruit of a mature and disenchanted realism (and the disenchantment has to be understood if the maturity of this stance is to be seen in its fullness and complexity):

> When we have finished quarrelling for crumbs
> Under the table, or gnawing the bones
> Of a dead culture, we will arise,
> Armed, but not in the old way.

It requires the clarity and integrity of a poet to state bluntly, in a period of political self-consciousness, the danger of 'gnawing' at a 'dead culture'. The disenchantment is still more acrid in the second poem, 'Welsh Landscape':

> There is no present in Wales,
> And no future;
> There is only the past;
> Brittle with relics.

The poet, even in lines which seem to appeal to the temper of
Glyndŵr, eschews the

> Wind-bitten towers and castles
> With sham ghosts,

and appears to be left here with

> an impotent people
> Sick with inbreeding,
> Worrying the carcase of an old song.

This apparent rejection is in fact no negative stance but a necessary
clear-sightedness which insists that no national regeneration can be
founded on false mythology; the more passionately R.S. Thomas
has pleaded for Wales and her resuscitation, the more he has insisted
on an honest analysis of her assumptions. If in a position of bogus
mythology 'there is no present in Wales' (and hence, tragically, 'no
future'), for the poet there *is* a present in his immediate environment,
in the harshness of the soil's sustenance and the movement of the
seasons. The peasant is no heir to the legends and impelled by no
old romanticism. His impulses are organic and the poet records (in
'Summer') the rhythm of the dour hill farmer from the frozen winter
'impotent with snow' to the response of his 'ascetic form' as his blood
'uncurls with the slow sap' and 'he meets himself', not in the legendary
past or an insecure future, but

> Everywhere in the smell of the ripe earth.

In a number of poems in *An Acre of Land* there is a new
qualification of his fastidious distrust of peasant harshness and
insensitivity. This is heard at its ironic clearest in 'Enigma' (the irony
directed not at the peasant but at the poet). It would appear that
the worker in the fields is deaf to bird-song, blind to the 'flower-
printed book of nature'. But the poem's conclusion is uncomfortable
for the sophisticated:

> Blind? Yes, and deaf, and dumb, and the last irks most,
> For could he speak, would not the glib tongue boast
> A love denied our neoteric sense,
> Being handed down from the age of innocence?

The deliberate clumsiness of 'neoteric' (when 'new' or 'modern' would have served) eases us into the quite surprising equation of the peasant with the 'noble savage' from 'the age of innocence', a rare concept indeed in Thomas's verse but appropriate here as a foil to the poet's sophistication. Nor is this more comfortable conclusion the end of the matter; for in 'The Labourer' there is a further ambiguous turn in the argument:

> What do you see?. . .
> A wild tree still, whose seasons are not yours,
> The slow heart beating to the hidden pulse
> Of the strong sap, the feet firm in the soil?
> No, no, a man like you, but blind with tears
> Of sweat to the bright star that draws you on.

Are we to read the final line as a true antithesis or is there a still further twist of irony in 'the bright star', the poet's goal?

This is a dark, ambivalent volume, full of checks and balances of tone and theme, with a calculated avoidance of clear conclusions. The reader is held in an uncomfortable suspension of judgement and there must have been for some a momentary relief in the more unambiguous clarity of the small masterpiece that followed a year later (1952), the dramatic poem for radio broadcasting, *The Minister*. There is a sustained anger in this poem which places it alongside the great classical satires. It should be read with the poem published six years later in *Poetry for Supper* and which could serve as an epigraph to the longer work:

> Who put that crease in your soul,
> Davies, ready this fine morning
> For the staid chapel where the Book's frown
> Sobers the sunlight. . .
> Who taught you your deft poise?

The covert 'democratic' tyranny of the 'deacons' over the young and visionary minister is the simple subject of the poem (its formal epigraph is the line of Welsh verse: '*Sŵn y galon fach yn torri*') and the whole work delicately explores the latent tragedy of a religious ethic divorced both from liturgy and rite and from the rhythms of daily life, by which men like Morgan, the minister, are

Condemned to wither and starve in the cramped cell
Of thought their fathers made them.

The setting for *The Minister* is the familiar terrain of all Thomas's early poetry, 'the hill country at the moor's edge', the home of 'the unchristened wind' and 'the inhuman cry of buzzards circling'. This is

> The marginal land where flesh meets spirit
> Only on Sundays and the days between
> Are mortgaged to the grasping soil.

The Reverend Elias Morgan, BA, is no Dylan Thomas character. He is the chosen pastor, picked 'as they chose their horses, / For hard work' — but his young ears are tuned more delicately than theirs. The singing of a loud thrush troubled his mind

> With strange theories, pagan but sweet,
> That made the Book's black letters dance
> To a tune John Calvin never heard.

This story has none of the subtle striving of the country priest, attempting to graft a rich tradition of liturgy and creed upon a tough upland stock; this is the struggle of a bitter casuistry picking its way between tact and truth:

> Although I never pried, I knew it all...
> And they knew I knew and pretended I didn't.

The core of the poet's satiric invective is not revealed until the last movement of the drama and it is left to the objectivity of the Narrator. To the sharp rhetoric of his question 'Is there no passion in Wales?' the poem gives the most explicit, most unambiguous answer:

> Protestantism — the adroit castrator
> Of art; the bitter negation
> Of song and dance and the heart's innocent joy —
> You have botched our flesh and left us only the soul's
> Terrible impotence in a warm world.

The minister has been defeated and the poem appears to end with his vain and wasteful death. But here R. S. Thomas presents us once more with one of his characteristic turns of argument, appearing to realign and modify the central movement of the poem. We have been led to compassion for the heroic struggle of a prophetic soul. But he had in fact been mistaken in the conditions of his struggle, choosing tragically to fight with that 'which yields to nothing human', least of all to rhetorical denunciation:

> He never listened to the hills'
> Music calling to the hushed
> Music within; but let his mind
> Fester with brooding on the sly
> Infirmities of the hill people.

And so he dies without realizing the ultimate wiping out of man's small aberrations. The closing lines of the poem express Thomas's own hardly-won knowledge of these matters, of the patient letting-be, the quiet waiting upon the generous liturgy of the natural order. For tragically, the minister had been mistaken in his stance:

> Wrong from the start, for nature's truth
> Is primary and her changing seasons
> Correct out of a vaster reason
> The vague errors of the flesh.

Once again R. S. Thomas has maintained the rhetorical poise which is the central characteristic of his verse, a poise which consists of a precise placing of opposed and seemingly irreconcilable truths. A work for broadcasting which appeared to originate in a satiric exploration of aspects of Protestant Nonconformity expands into far wider significances, into a compassionate writing of the heart's affections and their denial in greed and lust, of the imperatives of a moral order sanctioned by 'the Book' and the deeper imperatives of the natural order and the astringency of the seasons. To correct error is, within Thomas's universe, a matter of deft navigation, of preserving and articulating ancient truths, about man and his deep needs for worship and about Wales as the setting of his struggle. And because his universe — of Wales — is so confined, little more than an acre of land, the struggle and the poet's own deft poise are so clearly seen, so apparently lucid and yet so deeply ambivalent and disturbing.

21

The Minister was collected in the volume *Song at the Year's Turning* in 1955 which, with its selection from *The Stones of the Field* and *An Acre of Land* and with a perceptive introduction by John Betjeman, finally established R. S. Thomas's reputation. The handful of 'Later Poems' with which the volume concluded significantly underline the old themes, especially the 'matter of Wales', and also begin to open up new attitudes.

Prytherch is now a rich farmer whose growth in wealth has denied bird-song in April; the 'Village' is a small support against the world but now a new dimension enlarges the reference, for the world which revolves about the village is

> vast
> And meaningful as any poised
> By great Plato's solitary mind.

Coleridge is twice appealed to and Shelley dreamed the 'Song at the Year's Turning'; and this pattern of literary reference is one that will grow more complex with each succeeding volume.

Two extensions of insight finally establish this volume as an important landmark. After all the statement and counter-statement that have constituted the sustained argument on nature and the peasant in the earlier work and which provide a tacit, unspoken conclusion, one poem here, 'Autumn on the Land', appears for the moment to put a period to the argument. For, without reprehension, in even words, he poses a question:

> A man, a field, silence — what is there to say?

and disconcertingly gives two answers which have none of his customary ambiguity, no longer poised on the edge of decision:

> Beauty, love and mirth
> And joy are strangers there,

and the poem concludes with lines that appear final and indeed to qualify much of his earlier position:

> You must revise
> Your bland philosophy of nature, earth
> Has of itself no power to make men wise.

22

Taken in conjunction with their complementary statement in the closing words of *The Minister*, these lines represent the furthest point his argument has hitherto ventured, a conclusion which would have filled Wordsworth with a profound unease.

At the same time these last poems include two which are in the central metaphysical tradition, each a simple conceit developed with the most economic brevity. Together they constitute the only reminder in this collected volume that the intellectual argument I have tried to isolate is conducted within the terrain of the pastoral ministry of a priest who has his own vision to realize, while at the same time attempting to mediate it to a people lacking the vocabulary and indeed the sensibility to respond. The first, 'Pisces', must be quoted in its entirety and without comment, for it bears within the fragility of its minimal and masterly form all the tensions of the orders of being within which the poet moves, mythical, natural and divine:

> Who said to the trout,
> You shall die on Good Friday
> To be food for a man
> And his pretty lady?
>
> It was I, said God,
> Who formed the roses
> In the delicate flesh
> And the tooth that bruises.

The second poem, 'In a Country Church', has already been noted as the setting of R. S. Thomas's bitterest struggles with himself, where despite all prayer and the presence of the symbols of traditional beauty and grace, 'no word came'. But this is no more than a moment in the struggle; words may be denied (a severe enough deprivation for a poet-parson) but there is nonetheless the vision which passionately illuminates and fulfils the complex pattern of feeling and thought:

> Was he balked by silence? He kneeled long,
> And saw love in a dark crown
> Of thorns blazing, and a winter tree
> Golden with fruit of a man's body.

This is a poem that silences the rhetorical argument and leaves us at what we instinctively feel to be the heart of the poetry. And yet

23

in the last few pages, I have constantly used the words 'argument' and 'rhetoric' (in its fundamental sense of 'persuasion') and indeed Thomas himself has referred in *Words and the Poet* (The W. D. Thomas Memorial Lecture, 1964) to a central characteristic he recognized in his own work:

> There is always lurking at the back of my poetry a kind of moralistic or propagandist intention,

and in an important critical article in *Wales* in 1946 ('Some Contemporary Scottish Writing') he gives a fuller and more delicate statement of his aims:

> It is a formidable task this winnowing and purifying of the people. . . . The poet's chief problem is, how in virtue of his mind and vision can he best save his country — directly through political action, or indirectly through his creative work?

If there can be such a literary phenomenon as 'pure poetry', then R. S. Thomas's 'purity' as a poet seems compromised by his dual role as priest and self-conscious Welshman within a particular historical context; he assumes — demands — the old and honourable role of 'unacknowledged legislator' for the poet. This is of course no compromise but the source and strength of his content and of his peculiarly personal tone. This can be seen most clearly by examining a little more closely the commitment of his poetry to the social and political dilemmas of Wales.

IV

The W.D. Thomas Lecture, *Words and the Poet*, contains the bald statement, 'The two things that appeal most strongly to my imagination are Wales and nature' — and, as we shall see later, his 'Wales' is a society that looks back to an unspoiled nature before the impact of the Industrial Revolution and the growth of towns. In those earlier poems on Wales we have already seen, the necessary preparation for any 'propagandist intention' has been to adopt the dual stance of a romantic understanding of the Welsh, focused upon resonant names, Glyndŵr and the bards; and a bitter disenchant-ment with that romanticism when it became impotent for action. There appears a compound of shame and weariness in the occasional spurting invective ('sick with inbreeding, gnawing the bones of a dead culture, worrying the carcase of an old song') and this would seem an uncomfortable stance from which to contemplate a literary crusade on behalf of a nation. It is complicated by the question of language and its use as a literary medium. As early as 1946, in the article in *Wales*, 'Some Contemporary Scottish Writing', Thomas laid down the conditions for integrity within the choice of alternative media:

> There, too, is the dilemma of the so-called Anglo-Welsh writers... Are they, then, to be the instruments of the final capitulation of their country, or of 'an enlargement of national consciousness'? And if of the latter, how best can they achieve it, directly through political action, or indirectly through a literary movement? We have to face the possibility not, I think, of the disappearance of Welsh, but of its inadequacy as a medium for expressing the complex phantasmagoria of modern life. But if we choose English as that medium, have we the singleness of mind, the strength of will to remain primarily Welshmen? Ireland has done it, Scotland is striving after it, and we should do the same.

25

His own work has of course amply answered that question of the relation of a language to a nation's 'culture'. His very topic in the article in *Wales* places in focus that most confounding analogy to our Welsh situation, the existence of a lively Scottish poetry in English. Despite the splendid Gaelic of Sorley Maclean's poetry, mediated for us by his own translations and those of Iain Crichton Smith, and for all the unique and towering genius of Hugh MacDiarmid communicating in large part in an essentially literary artefact, the language of poetry in Scotland is the English of Norman MacCaig and Edwin Morgan. Yet this does little to reduce the emotional and intellectual pressure upon the writer who is impelled to choose English as his medium within the Welsh context. This has produced an enriching internal tension within R. S. Thomas's poetry and with its gradual resolution (this particular tension has diminished in the more recent volumes) there has been more creative energy to spare for the profounder topic explored in the same article in *Wales*. Since 1946 his sense of his 'formidable task' which he then defined as 'the winnowing and purifying of the people', has become subtler and more manifold; but the programme was clear and its source and impulsive drive quite clear at that date. He identifies the dilemma of the poet, posed by the pressures of 'his mind and vision', as the choice of method by which his country can best be redeemed — through 'political action' or 'his creative work'. For R. S. Thomas the dilemma is not that of Matthew Arnold for whom poetry took over the role of theology; Thomas is too clear-sighted to confuse the moral, theological and imaginative roles and his poetry is about the business of sharpening sensibility, of focusing discrimination. By the astringency of the poet's attitudes (he would agree here with Edward Bond that 'Imagination is one / Of the exact sciences'), the bogus is winnowed from the true and those elements that make for life and enrichment are distinguished from those which atrophy the mind and the heart. That this is inseparable from his theological concerns is of course clear but the distinction between them is nonetheless valid and necessary. Though his phrase in *Words and the Poet* concerning his constant 'moralistic or propagandist intention' is both summary and crude, he clearly places himself in the line of Plato, Sidney, Johnson and Arnold; working by oblique indirection and with increasing subtlety in the recent volumes, R. S. Thomas makes his intellectual, social and political commitments abundantly clear.

This, then, is the background to his poems of Welsh concern. Up to the publication of *Song at the Year's Turning* (1955) his attitudes were best clarified in the two poems, 'Welsh History' and 'A Welshman to any Tourist'. The former has already been seen in another context and is an ironic conspectus of histrionic attitudes:

> our lean bellies
> And our mud houses were a proof
> Of our ineptitude for life;

but however vainly we might gnaw at the bones of a dead culture, the final conviction is of a renewed national consciousness, 'armed but not in the old way'. The second poem is more suavely ironic. The tourist in Wales will face none of the vastnesses of America:

> We've nothing to offer you, no deserts
> Except the waste of thought
> Forming from mind erosion.

The scale is the scale of hills, 'fine, of course, / And bearded with water to suggest age' and the whole withdrawn remoteness turning upon legend, Arthur and his knights, 'the bright ore / That seams our history', waiting to come to the aid of Wales:

> But shame has kept them late in bed.

After the garnering of *Song at the Year's Turning*, the way was open for the advances we find in *Poetry for Supper* (1958). The long poem, 'Border Blues', with which the collection opens, extends the wit of its title with a very varied irony. The old cultural counters are deftly placed — 'Oliver in nylons', 'Arthur leers' and 'Ysbaddaden Penkawr's cunning' is outmatched by the peasant woman at her kitchen table. The border is the meeting-place of two derelictions, the English, seen with a wry twist:

> Blue eyes and Birmingham yellow
> Hair, and the ritual murder of vowels,

while the Welsh farm labourer, going to Shrewsbury for his second-hand pleasures ('It was "The Babes" this year, all about nature') is seen at work with the earlier brutality:

27

Rising early
To flog the carcase
Of the brute earth.

The whole picture, set within the tragic fact of rural depopulation,
is made wryly irreverent by the quotation:

We are not English...Ni bydd diwedd
Byth ar sŵn y delyn aur.

This mode of irony marks the new assurance which can extend to
a frank acknowledgement of the poet's groping towards a vision.
'Temptation of a Poet' honestly confesses the lure of the customary
theme,

To make tryst with the pale ghost
Of an earlier self,

and even to recreate a Prytherch in the old image. But the endeavour
in this new volume is to be with new concerns, even if they are only
dimly seen:

But the mind draws
Me onward blind with the world's dust,
Seeking a spring that my heart fumbles.

This expresses clearly one of the most engaging aspects of
R. S. Thomas's work, the sense of 'work (and thought) in progress'.
He is never afraid to declare that a poem is 'interim', on the way
to a firmer position. Some whole volumes of his work have been
of this kind; others, notably *Frequencies*, published in 1978, give the
impression of a conclusion reached, a worked-out position. Yet this
whole rhythm in his creative life ensures that these works of apparent
finality are 'definitive' only for the moment, a secure basis for new
development. In this sense *Poetry for Supper* expresses a new sureness
and maturity in his contemplation of his pastoral ministry, his
priesthood and its relation to his verse. He can now venture to look
at this ministry and its point of greatest apparent failure, its inability
to comfort the countryman in his sombre home:

It was not the dark filling my eyes
and mouth appalled me . . .

28

It was the dark
Silting the veins of that sick man
I left stranded upon the vast
And lonely shore of his bleak bed.

This humble confession of perhaps inevitable failure (every priest will understand him) accompanies the contrasted pictures of two vigorous representatives of his flock, 'The Muck Farmer' with whom no contact can be made, the relationship ending in tragic disparity:

Our ways have crossed and tend now apart;
Ours to end in a field wisely sown,
His in the mixen of his warped heart;

and, wholly different in its tone:

O, hers is all
This strong body, this safe island
Where men may come, sons and lovers,
Daring the cold seas of her eyes,

the cool appraisal achieving a portrait full of affectionate admiration. And with a sharp shock, almost of affront, we reach the central poem of this volume, which locks together the dilemmas of the country parson, his frustrated aspirations for the people entrusted to him, his awareness of his own vision clouded by the facts of his daily ministrations and the hope that they may somehow be reconciled in a wider purpose. For 'Country Clergy' is a passionately honest poem. It has its ancient grace:

I see them working in old rectories
By the sun's light, by candlelight,
Venerable men,

but the core of the poem concerns their 'lonely thought in grey parishes', that on country minds and hearts they wrote 'sublime words / Too soon forgotten'. The central lines are shocking in their direct expression of distinction in words which few priests would dare to think — much less articulate:

And yet their skulls,
Ripening over so many prayers,
Toppled into the same grave
With oafs and yokels.

29

In its acceptance of a cool uncharity, a mode of confession, of purgation, the poem earns the right to its closing affirmation:

> God in his time
> Or out of time will correct this.

Complementary poems to 'The Country Clergy' transform our understanding of his archetypal countryman, Iago Prytherch. They themselves make a strange pair of poems. The first, 'Green Categories', places Iago in a most unaccustomed setting:

> You never heard of Kant, did you, Prytherch?

It is a beautifully distanced exploration of the world of genius, of the 'remote war of antinomies' on the one hand, and on the other the total sureness of things 'rooted in the flesh, / Stone, tree and flower'. Each member of the equation is confounded, Kant's logic failing before the recalcitrant facts and Prytherch faltering through sudden exposure 'to the cold wind of genius'. Yet, startlingly, Thomas sees them reconciled and Iago Prytherch raised to a wholly unwonted dignity (and Kant perhaps elevated to a new insight):

> Yet at night together
> In your small garden, fenced from the wild moor's
> Constant aggression, you could have been at one,
> Sharing your faith over a star's blue fire.

The second poem, 'Absolution', is more overtly pastoral in the professional sense. For the first time the priest feels confounded by the peasant's endurance:

> Prytherch, man, can you forgive?

and, with sad reversal of roles, contrasts the stark field:

> Your stone altar on which the light's
> Bread is broken at dusk and dawn

with his own fate:

> While I have worn my soul bare
> On the world's roads.

30

The reversal of ministry is maintained to the end, in which the priest finds,

> With the slow lifting up of your hand
> No welcome, only forgiveness.

There is in fact a third poem here, called simply 'Iago Prytherch', but this leads more properly into another new and important preoccupation of this volume, the poet's own craft. In this poem Thomas finds it necessary to identify precisely his attitude to Iago:

> Made fun of you? That was their graceless
> Accusation because I took
> Your rags for theme, because I showed them
> Your thought's bareness . . .
> Fun? Pity? No word can describe
> My true feelings.

The confounding confrontation of priest and countryman, of poet with subject, is revealed as the spring of his creativity. This 'dark figure' is a 'gaunt question', while

> My poems were made in its long shadow
> Falling coldly across the page.

We hear little of the poet's craft in earlier collections but in the poem for which this volume is named the conditions of the craft are spelled out:

> 'Natural, hell! What was it Chaucer
> Said once about the long toil
> That goes like blood to the poem's making?'

and there is wry acceptance in his admission:

> Man, you must sweat
> And rhyme your guts taut, if you'd build
> Your verse a ladder.

And if he is clear about the discipline of verse, this volume also reaches a further clarity on 'the matter of Wales', in two poems that overtly treat the poet's vocation. 'Composition' explains the themes, 'of the tears of men too long dead', of truth:

                              but the pen's scalpel tip
          Was too sharp;

he tried love, and 'slowly the blood congealed'. From this dark
conclusion Thomas turns to his central poetic vocation in 'The Cure'.
Here the poet is consciously a 'doctor in verse',

              Whose rough hands manipulate
              The fine bones of a sick culture

and we are back with the poet's necessary burden of 'winnowing
and purifying the people'. Sharply he is confronted with his vocation
— 'What to do?':

                    Consider, you...
              What areas of that infirm body
              Depend solely on a poet's cure.

R. S. Thomas has a curious affinity here with two older poets of very
differing manner, Pound and MacDiarmid; in his prose and more
pungently in the 'Usura' Cantos, Ezra Pound diagnosed the greed
which was in his judgement the cancer of contemporary society in
the West; in *A Drunk Man Looks at the Thistle* and beyond, Hugh
MacDiarmid, with more flexible satiric weapons, mocks the more
bogus attitudes of contemporary Scotland. No community enjoys
the manipulative surgery involved in this order of poetic analysis,
and R. S. Thomas is in distinguished company in speaking out of
the heart of tradition while still critical of it; as he has himself said,
'Some immature people think that if you criticise them you hate
them. People find it difficult to believe you can be at once critical
and compassionate.'
    We shall have to return to this concern with the condition of Wales
in later verse; we need now to explore a complementary topic, the
culture of cities, first opened as an explicit topic in this volume:

              And to be able to put at the end
              Of this letter, Athens, Florence.
                                        ('The Letter')

R. S. Thomas has always been disconcertingly ambivalent on the
subject of cities and the distinctiveness of their culture. City-bred

                              32

and classically trained, he has no doubt about the values of civilization and their source; equally his own particular urbanity, the steady values of one for whom the country is not inherited and in the blood but adopted and sedulously cultivated, has demonstrated itself even when he has appeared most vigorously to reject the urban values.

City names and their reverberations have here a special significance, while the relationship between a city and its hinterland is delicately but effectively seen in a relatively late poem, 'Burgos', in *Not That He Brought Flowers* (1968). The name, rich in associations, is the axis of the poem, yet apart from the title the city is scarcely mentioned but is located in the imagination by its surrounding countryside, tributary and impoverished. The poem opens deceptively:

> Nightingales crackled in the frost
> At Burgos.

The twin blessings of beauty and refreshing cold are denied in every succeeding line of the poem. 'The day dawned fiercely', the land is 'parched', the fields are no ideal countryside but 'bitter with sage and thistles'. And religion, the core of the ideal city of antiquity, is here a tragic disillusion, while every adjective ('lonely', 'sad', 'lost') emphasizes the desolation:

> Lonely bells called
> From the villages; no one answered
> Them but the sad priests, fingering
> Their beads, praying for the lost people
> Of the soil.

The beneficent symbiosis of town and country is here wholly denied and the poem ends in tragic rejection:

> In the air an eagle
> Circled, shadowless as the God
> Who made that country and drinks its blood.

This is an admirably wrought poem, tensely controlled in feeling but concerned with the tragic doings of man with man and the destruction of their environment. On other occasions this concern

33

produces a curious prosaic shrillness, as in the article in *Wales* in 1948 in which he gives 'A Welsh View of the Scottish Renaissance':

> You must forgive me if I rant but I hate towns and so-called modern civilisation and all they stand for.

Now this clearly will not do, even for R. S. Thomas, and his own uneasy reserve is betrayed in the opening phrase. Nor do we get this heightened tone in the poetry. To return to the poem, 'The Letter', in *Poetry for Supper*, we have the careful choice of Athens and Florence as the address of the letter, names noble in themselves and expressing in a cultivated shorthand the axis of civilization, the twin poles of philosophy and art. The poem is in no way oblique in its implications; rather it is unwontedly specific. To have reached Athens and Florence is to have arrived at the end of the legendary journey of the spirit through the perilous places and dark ways:

> ...Athens, Florence — some name
> That the spirit recalls from earlier journeys
> Through the dark wood, seeking the path
> To the bright mansions.

And to this myth of the soul's progress is added the gloss; that the 'bright mansions' are those 'cities and towns / Where the soul added depth to its stature'. This is a far cry from the child in 'The Evacuee' (*An Acre of Land*), who became a cherished 'bird in the nest' of the countryside,

> Home now after so long away
> In the flowerless streets of the drab town.

We are faced with the simple contradiction which Shakespeare explored in *As You Like It*: the city and the court are both the source of civilized values and the locus of corruption; the countryside is the repository of pastoral values, a place of renewal and refreshment and of toil so severe as to degrade the toiler. Between the two there is a necessary rhythm, most movingly expressed by R. S. Thomas in one of his rare creative pieces in prose, his nativity meditation in *Wales* (December, 1959):

> It is the sense of harmony of town and country which is so much a part of the Nativity. Mary, like a farm wife, comes into the town to give birth to her child, the town that is the summit of man's

achievement, the city that he builds to the glory of God. And the shepherds come in from the fields to see the great wonder that has occurred, symbols of that flowing in of food and inspiration and re-invigoration without which all towns must wither and die. And there they find Christ, a sign of God's blessing upon the town as the focus of civilisation.

This is nobly said and adjusts our opinion of his customary exploration of the country as a place of refreshment and re-creation. The vision of the *Eclogues*, of the City State, of the rhythm between the prophetic uplands of Judah and the destiny of Jerusalem, have all gone to the making of this meditation; and its terms are unmistakable: 'the town . . . the summit of man's achievement . . . to the glory of God . . . the focus of civilisation'. Thomas may well have valued Scottish writers for their rebellion against 'the English urban and mechanised civilisation' but he recognizes that this is rebellion against an aberration, a denial of the nature of the city. Though the very great bulk of his poetry is concerned with the country and the countryman, it is also just to say that the verse makes clear his conviction that it is not the city only that can be betrayed by its inhabitants; the country knows a similar treachery, the dumb sternness of its life so often turning the peasant into an unthinking, almost an unfeeling, animal. And if it is in the nature of the city to deteriorate into corruption and become parasitic on the countryside, the countryside in turn has its own in-built principle of cruelty and of attrition upon its inhabitants.

V

When he is exploring the work of other poets to make anthologies of their poems, R. S. Thomas seems drawn first to poets of theological insight (as in his edition of George Herbert and in the *Penguin Anthology of Religious Verse*); or he is led instinctively to the 'nature poets' like Wordsworth and Edward Thomas. In his selection from the latter for the Faber series (1964), he writes:

> It was in the few books on subjects dear to him that Thomas's true self appeared. In works such as 'The Heart of England', 'The Country' and 'The South Country' he wrote happily of his wanderings among the lanes, and on the downs of the south of England. His taste was for solitude, the quiet observation of birds, beasts and flowers but salted always by chance conversations with the early inhabitants of the country through which he passed. These books are a prelude, though a significant one, to the poetry that was to come.

R. S. Thomas also is a solitary, devoting much of his time to the observation of bird-life on Llŷn. Yet in his poetry — so often more precisely acute in its generalization than his prose — he is prepared to qualify this instinctive turn to country sources and away from the city. We have seen this as early as *Song at the Year's Turning* (1958); in the poem 'Autumn on the Land' he not only declares that

> History is made
> Elsewhere: the hours forfeit to time's blade
> Don't matter here,

but there is a profound poverty of spirit among its inhabitants:

> Beauty, love and mirth
> And joy are strangers there,

36

for, in the unremitting struggle with earth and elements,

> The thin, shy soul has not begun its reign
> Over the darkness.

This is a customary concept throughout his poetry, implied in so many peasant portraits. But, as we have seen, the final generalization is unusually sharp in its definition, for earth

> Has of itself no power to make men wise.

It is left to a later volume, *Young and Old*, published in 1972 in the Chatto series of 'Poets for the Young', to express his most complex statement of this qualification of nature's beneficence. It is a disconcerting volume to be aimed at the young reader and one of its most disconcerting poems is 'Horizons'. The initial stance seems both traditional and unusually 'lyrical':

> What beauty! The green silk
> Of water, stretched tight over
> The rocks, so that one can see
> The fishes pilfering the brown
> Orchards.

Despite the unusual metaphor the tone is even; but it changes sharply and unexpectedly:

> Such thoughts trouble
> Me; the calm kingdom
> Of nature is too pure
> To inhabit.

The apparent irony in the last phrase is finally qualified in a convoluted verse-sentence whose assertions turn upon themselves, both extending and reversing their argument with all the sharp antithesis of the opening stanza:

> I look beyond
> It always to a cruel shore
> Of horror, where men fight
> And destroy, not innocently
> As beasts do, but with the mind's

37

Trophies and the spirit's
Consciously in their care.

At least four times the thought movement here arrests and qualifies itself. The calm purity of nature is looked through to a 'cruel shore of horror' in which man's warfare is contrasted with the beasts' slaying innocently for food or territory; with the introduction of 'mind's trophies' there would appear to be the implication that calculated thought upon aggression — by contrast with the instinctive violence of the beast — is the source of corruption and of the poet's horror; but in the closing lines the 'mind's trophies' are linked to the 'spirit's' and in the final ambiguity of the word 'care', the previous, apparently condemnatory comparison of man with beast seems to be reversed. Unlike nature's, man's struggle is not simply for survival (however innocent that struggle may be) but for the preservation of hard-won symbols ('trophies') of mind and spirit which are the products of civilization.

Here then is a pattern of antitheses, of man and nature, of the values of the land and of the culture of cities, of innocence and urbanity, which are never resolved in the poetry. Nor can they be. It is a tension which has traversed our culture and been the source of a great deal of our art; it is no small part of R. S. Thomas's poised craft that he renews the ancient argument with such conscious understanding of its implications and without stultifying commitment to either side. Indeed the only comforting resolution of these manifold antitheses would appear to be that we evaluate and criticize the values of life on the land by precisely those urbane values derived from the city, 'that summit of man's achievement', an achievement which in turn demands refreshment and purification (Thomas's terms are 'inspiration and re-invigoration') by contact with the natural order of things, the rhythms of the seasons and the elements.

VI

The publication of *Tares* in 1961 appeared to mark a pause, a gathering-in of the poet's work. It is an unassertive volume, seemingly mulling over the customary themes; but they are extended and amplified in a handful of poems which show a poise, a sureness of argument which is the fruit of a new maturity. The success of *Song at the Year's Turning* is now being reaped in a greater relaxation and an absence of assertive self-consciousness. He finds no need for an aggressive rhetoric and in a poem from the earlier volume, *Poetry for Supper*, he anticipates this new direction.

'Death of a Poet' is Thomas's most clear-toned statement of a poet's choices. The world waits on the dying poet's last words, his ultimately valid craftsman's testament; but there is 'just the one word "sorry" '; forgiveness is begged for the artist's failure in his vocation:

> Sorry for the lies, for the long failure
> In the poet's war; that he preferred
> The easier rhythms of the heart
> To the mind's scansion.

Nor are his choices solely those of 'heart' and 'mind'; there are the more bitter decisions within the vocation, leading to the conviction

> that now he dies
> Intestate, having nothing to leave
> But a few songs, cold as stones
> In the thin hands that asked for bread.

The theme is taken up in a central poem in *Tares*. 'Those Others' is printed with an epigraph from Dewi Emrys:

> A gofid gwerin gyfan
> Yn fy nghri fel taerni tân.
> (A whole folk's sorrow in my fire-urgent cry.)

39

The relationship of the 'rhythms of the heart' and 'the mind's scansion' in this later poem attaches to the familiar themes of race, country and soil. The poet tries to calculate his role in his land, why, with so many fertile places that destiny might have chosen for him, 'the cramped womb' of Wales should have been the place of his conception. This brooding involves an examination of the slow-growing hate which at last focuses on his 'own kind':

> For men of the Welsh race
> Who brood with dark face
> Over their thin navel
> To learn what to sell.

There had been a possible alternative object of his rejection, 'the brute earth'; but this did not attract his hatred, for

> That is strong here and clean
> And plain in its meaning
> As none of the books are
> That tell of the war
>
> Of heart with head, leaving
> The wild birds to sing
> The best songs.

In the earlier poem 'heart' and 'head' had been opposed instruments of sensibility; there 'the war of heart with head', the tension of instinct against thought, inheres in man's condition by unfortunate comparison with 'brute earth'; the poet, involved in the human tension and divorced from earth, concedes victory to the birds who sing a more spontaneous song. This concern with the two ways of knowledge (an almost Lawrentian dichotomy of blood and mind), comes to no calculated and inevitable conclusion in R. S. Thomas. In 'Death of a Poet' there is clearly a bias towards 'the mind's scansion' against 'the easier rhythms of the heart'; in 'Those Others' they form a conjoined category opposed to natural rhythms.

A second poem in Poetry for Supper which anticipates new developments in Tares is 'The Journey'. Here we have a confrontation with a man 'whose eyes declare: There is no God'. There are many replies possible to him and his fellows but the ultimate reply is the journey itself, the ascent:

        the road runs on
With many turnings towards the tall
Tree to which the believer is nailed.

The *pietà*, the divine body in the maid's arms, is a recurrent theme
in his work, to which we must return; in this poem the changed
image is powerful: the believer and not the object of belief is crucified.
The unexpected fulfilment of this conception in *Tares* is associated
with a new stature for Iago Prytherch (in 'The Dark Well', the opening
poem of the collection) and — strange conjunction — with the art
of Fritz Kreisler.

    Iago Prytherch here reaches a final status as the poet's mentor;
no longer 'a poor farmer with no name', he is now one

        Who more than all directed my slow
        Charity where there was need.

Tragedy, dereliction, appears now to be the sole answer to man's twin
needs, here simply categorized:

        There are two hungers, hunger for bread
        And hunger of the uncouth soul
        For the light's grace.

This seems to reflect a familiar antithesis, of peasant and sophisticate,
of blunt and subtle perception of need. But a kind of crucifixion
has been experienced and Prytherch — rather than the poet — has
taught charity precisely because his

                heart, fuller than mine
        Of gulped tears, is the dark well
        From which to draw, drop after drop,
        The terrible poetry of his kind.

This recognition of the true relationship of peasant and priest gives
a new dignity to the poems in *Tares*.

    And lest this should be seen merely as a return to those whose
roots are essentially in earth, R. S. Thomas explores the same intuition
in a field nearer his vocation as a poet, in 'The Musician'. It is a
commonplace enough occasion, unpretentiously recorded; the poet
in a crowded recital by Kreisler is pushed among the audience on
the stage,

41

> So near that I could see the toil
> Of his face muscles.

But he could see more, and this prepares us in part for the startling conjunction with which the poem closes; for he was near enough to see behind the play of muscle that the violinist

> so beautifully suffered
> For each of us upon his instrument.

The opening of the third stanza, despite this hint, still shocks:

> So it must have been on Calvary
> In the fierce light of the thorn's halo,

and the analogy is pursued quite simply, to the audience standing by:

> and that one figure,
> The hands bleeding, the mind bruised but calm.

The preoccupation with crucifixion is central to Thomas's creed; not until this understated volume is it linked with the destiny of the artist's passion, calm and controlled.

This collection carries — as so often with R. S. Thomas's works — an explanatory epigraph:

> Didst not thou sow good seed in thy field?
> From whence, then, hath it tares?
> St Matthew 13:27

The corruption of the good seed and the marring of the field by tares is the unstressed theme of the whole volume and the source of its restraint — one walks delicately, prizing and cherishing every value, for it is vulnerable. Two subjects are relatively new in this collection and each carries a powerful emotional charge in this new context.

Few poets have spoken of intimate personal relationships with such restrained, almost cryptic, passion as R. S. Thomas. Earlier poems had spoken of the relationship of father and child, his son Gwydion; here, in 'Anniversary', he celebrates the more intimate relationship of marriage. The tenderness is reticent, almost to silence, with the small commonplaces, factual, yet symbols of deeper emotions:

42

Eating our bread,
Using the same air. . .
Keeping simple house.

The fastidious discrimination that characterizes R.S. Thomas's poetry
has its parallel in the strong delicacy of the landscapes, the minute
bird-studies painted and drawn by his wife, Elsie (M.R. Eldridge).
And it is this fastidious poise that he is prepared to reveal as the
'tone' of their marriage. The meal stands at the heart of the
relationship, the food more than shared:

> We balance it thoughtfully
> On the tip of the tongue,
> Careful to maintain
> The strict palate.

It is a profoundly moving poem, precisely because it sets aside overt
emotion and speaks so clearly of a shared and critical discrimination.

The second, long familiar theme, involves a brief return in two
poems to 'the matter of Wales'. Here the good seed could be over-
whelmed by the tares deplored in so many earlier poems. But the
tone in these poems is considered, argumentative, as in so much
in *Tares*. The first, 'Hyddgen', has as its subject-matter so many of
the old topics, Glyndŵr, ancient battles, the oblivion of history, the
shepherd and the land. But now the voice is laconic, the more marked
in the delicate undertone of the scriptural in the word 'hireling':

> Look at those sheep,
> On such small bones
> The best mutton,
> But not for him,
> The hireling shepherd.

Within the laconic goes a serene acceptance of history, a time-scale
that is no longer human, but the vaster leisure of nature's rhythms:

> History goes on;
> On the rock the lichen
> Records it: no mention
> Of them, of us.

The better-known — if less subtle — poem, 'A Welsh Testament', also realigns the former counters of argument but with some unexpected moves. Welshness is now wryly accepted ('All right, / I was Welsh') as an accident of time and place:

> I spoke the tongue that was passed on
> To me in the place I happened to be,

while the invoking of Glyndŵr has by this time its own reserved irony — 'What was descent from him?' — an irony extended to the God who was 'to have a peculiar care / For the Welsh people':

> History showed us
> He was too big to be nailed to the wall
> Of a stone chapel, yet still we crammed him
> Between the boards of a black book.

As the shepherd, reluctantly exhibiting his skills to the tourist, resists the mutation of Wales into a haven of peace — 'Is a museum Peace?' — so the poet now accepts

> the absurd label
> Of birth, of race hanging askew
> About my shoulders

without either pride or the shamed castigation which formerly he had reserved for the ills of his country. With whatever attentiveness he declares his Welshness, it is subordinate to his humanity, his priesthood, his vocation as poet:

> I am a man;
> I never wanted the drab rôle
> Life assigned me.

Finally, to round off its impression of a mature garnering of themes *Tares* has a brief, ambiguous and highly suggestive glimpse of the poet's craft in 'The Maker':

> He took pencil,
> The mind's cartridge, and blank paper,
> And drilled his thoughts to the slow beat
> Of the blood's drum.

The old antithesis of mind and blood is here resolved, disciplined to a single creative act, calculated even in its emotional throb. And there is the suggestion that the result of this craftsman's care is of wider, perhaps even of prophetic, significance; for as the poem formed itself on the clear surface of the paper, it

> went marching
> Onward through time, while the spent cities
> And dry hearts smoked in its wake.

Through the whole range of its subjects and their treatment, this unassertive volume declares greater, more daring, claims than any of its predecessors.

VII

Reviewers had done their best with the works hitherto, in a strange agglomeration of epithets: 'civilized, understanding and very intelligent', 'uncompromising as granite, sculptural but not cold', 'honest', 'vital', 'quiet, grim, laconic, resigned' — it all sounded rather forbidding, as though an ikon had found a voice; but R. S. Thomas was now established as a major writer and it was clear that the new volume, *The Bread of Truth* (1963), aroused unusual expectations, especially after the quiet garnering of the previous volume. Every reader makes his own devious way into a new collection of poems and my way into this book was the poem 'Souillac: le Sacrifice d'Abraham'. The carving of the sacrifice of Isaac in the church of Souillac is a vigorous and austere work, stylized almost to the point of anonymity. In the poem it becomes much more complex. First there is comment on the primitive rite, a comment which is a terse interpretation of a seemingly incomprehensible sacrifice:

> And he grasps him by the hair
> With innocent savagery.
> And the son's face is calm;
> There is trust there,

and the comment extends into the world of art:

> This is what art can do,
> Interpreting faith
> With serene chisel.

R. S. Thomas has himself earned the right to that adjective after years of discipline. His own engaged and yet objective poise has none of the neutrality of Eliot's 'poetic catalyst', unmoved while it creates, but the involvement in his finest poems has the serenity he attributes

46

to the anonymous sculptor. And finally there is the assured under-standing of the material, the stone as resistant as words:

> The recalcitrant stone
> Is quiet as our breath,
> And is accepted.

This secure economy, content to leave so much unsaid, so much scholarship and insight merely hinted at, characterizes the whole volume. In this clarity he is able to examine the vocation of priest with some finality and does so in three poems richer than any hitherto in his work: 'Country Cures', 'The Mill' and 'Servant'. The first of these poems has a curious aloofness, as though Thomas were not himself in charge of a country living:

> I know those places and the lean men
> Whose collars fasten them by the neck
> To loneliness; as I go by. . .

the picture set in the frame of 'their gaunt houses'. This emptiness, the human isolation, returns upon the priest who wishes to exercise his ministry with other human beings but finds he has been sent to the remote parish 'to learn patience', where the introverted ministry has one end:

> to make your soul
> In long hours by the poor light
> Of a few, pale leaves on a tree
> In autumn or a flower in spring.

This is autobiography with a rare and austere objectivity. 'The Mill' is one of the small handful of poems in which the acts of priesthood are themselves looked at. A miller, bed-ridden and 'lying log heavy', is for his family,

> one more beast
> To be fed and watered,

but despite the labour he is an occasion for compassion, fostering 'a seed of love' in 'a crack in their hearts'. To this family comes the ministering priest, to listen to him tell of 'old exploits / With the plough and scythe' and to declare the other reality:

> I read him the psalms,
> Said prayers and was still;

and for nine years,

> While the past's slow stream,
> Flowing through his head,
> Kept the rusty mill
> Of the mind turning —
> It was I it ground.

This poem is longer than Thomas's customary span and it gives him space to set the home, the dying man and the priest in their spiritual context, almost tonelessly, almost without comment beyond the harsh fact of the closing line. The term 'sacrificial priesthood' here takes on a new dimension, with its identification of a parson with his people in all their dereliction.

'Servant' is a complementary poem to 'The Mill', quite different in its comment on the priest's role; it is an acknowledgement of a debt, the generosity of which demands an understanding of the earlier poems on this subject. For this is a return to Iago Prytherch and the relation of their roles is now significantly shifted, as the poem fully declares.

But not without question. The opening lines of the poem acknowledge the priest's turning to Prytherch for his reading of 'the field's pages, the land's story', for the accurate insight proved not in the mind but 'in your bone and your blood'. And there is resistance:

> Is truth so bare,
> So dark, so dumb, as on your hearth
> And in your company I found it?

But this resistance carries none of the rejection that invited the acrid tone of similar subjects in the early volumes. Now there is a fuller acceptance of that which the poet learned from Prytherch, from the

> Seed sown upon the thin
> Soil of the heart, not rich, not fertile,
> Yet capable of the one crop,
> Which is the bread of truth I break.

48

It is much that Iago Prytherch provides the title to this volume of poetry; it is much more that the title is removed from the commonplace, even from the philosophical in its implications; for in the final words, 'I break', the relationship between priest and peasant is raised to the sacramental, 'in the breaking of bread'. This is 'the matter of Wales' with a splendid difference; and it returns strangely in the poem, 'On the Farm'. There were Dai, Llew and Huw Puw, all 'no good':

> And lastly there was the girl;
> Beauty under some spell of the beast.
> Her pale face was the lantern
> By which they read in life's dark book
> The shrill sentence: God is love.

In all their bizarre half-perceptions, this is not the first time that the men of the country have been redeemed by their womenkind, though here in another dimension.

Wales, too, in this collection, is seen in another perspective and through other eyes, those of his fellow poet Saunders Lewis, whose vision has been nearer the heart of the matter than any other artist in twentieth-century Wales. His presence is prefigured by Gwenallt in 'A Lecturer', a powerful tribute, the more powerful in its understatement, to this man 'keeping close to the wall / Of life':

> Not dangerous?
> He has been in gaol.

'The Patriot' acknowledges his more intimate debt to Saunders Lewis, perhaps one source of R. S. Thomas's fierce invective; for the older poet 'had that rare gift' that

> Even the simplest statement could inflame
> The mind and heart of the hearer,

and possessed that other talent, akin to the craft of the surgeon, that his words

> Opened again the concealed wounds
> Of history in the comfortable flesh.

Indeed the relationship between the work of Saunders Lewis and of R.S. Thomas is especially significant. For each of them history is a living thing, stirring in the blood; for each language is the communication of a tradition not confined to Wales but European-wide and millennia-long; neither has sought power or place; for each, poetry has expressed the same prophetic union of compassion with a cleansing anger. And it has to be confessed that the Wales of their contemporaries has found neither to be a comfortable fellow citizen. Truth is rarely mollifying.

We come full circle from Souillac with two poems addressed to poets; for it is significant that we find in this volume the two dominant themes of priesthood and the condition of Wales, framed within his concern for the status of art. 'To a Young Poet' is a gently ironic mirror held deprecatingly for his own gaze. For the first half of a poet's career there is no fulfilment beyond the necessary revelation that poetry is not a loving relationship with a Muse but 'a grave service / Of a cold queen' and when certainty comes in 'sad manhood', humility compels the realization that

> the smile
> On her proud face is not for you.

If this is an estimate by R.S. Thomas of his own work, no critic would agree with him; and yet in his austere world it may have a certain truth — if a smile is what he sought.

His poem to 'Wallace Stevens' is an astringent and perceptive examination of a major poet, again acknowledging a deep affinity. The words in verse go beyond any similar analysis in critical prose:

> he preferred black,
> The deep spaces between stars,
> Fathomless as the cold shadow
> His mind cast.

His recognition of Stevens's verse as 'dry leaves of a dry mind' and the closing perception of the bitter source of the poet's power,

> taking despair
> As a new antidote for love

50

demonstrates his own fearless critical intelligence. Though R. S. Thomas's subject matter may be calculatedly confined by a fastidious economy, the literary power behind the innate perceptiveness is the result of a classical intelligence as wide-ranging as any in the contemporary literary scene.

VIII

R. S. Thomas has given a splendid demonstration of the economy that can result from anthologizing oneself. *Selected Poems, 1946–1968*, published in 1973, chose work from the eight earlier volumes (for *Song at the Year's Turning* had already selected from *The Stones of the Field* and *An Acre of Land*, though the economy in the 1973 volume is even more stringent). Nowhere is the selection more revealing than in *Pietà* (first published in 1966), for the whole collection is represented by only ten poems, on closely related themes. With this volume the topic of Thomas's religious verse confronts us most urgently and it is perhaps best approached by way of his *Penguin Book of Religious Verse*, published three years earlier, in 1963. Roland Mathias, in a distinguished essay on 'Philosophy and Religion in the poetry of R. S. Thomas' (*Poetry Wales*, Spring 1972) points out that 'a glance at R. S. Thomas's own *Penguin Book of Religious Verse* (1963) will reveal with what latitude he could and did interpret the adjective "religious". Indeed, such a glance will puncture a little the surprise that might be felt on realising his own unorthodoxies.' These 'unorthodoxies' can be exaggerated and misunderstood but the provocative titles of the sections of the anthology (God, Self, Nothing, It, All) in themselves constitute a philosophy of religious verse and the brief introduction provides its rationale.

He feels it necessary first to justify the conjunction of religion with verse and he does so by way of Coleridge:

> The nearest we approach to God, he (Coleridge) appears to say, is as creative beings. The poet, by echoing the primary imagination, recreates. Through his work he forces those who read him to do the same, thus bringing them nearer the primary imagination themselves, and so, in a way, nearer to the actual being of God as displayed in action.

This is a familiar and acceptable argument but Thomas goes on to reveal the springs of so much in his own work when he explores despair as a spiritual condition, first in the 'terrible' sonnets of Gerard Manley Hopkins which 'are but a human repetition of the cry from the Cross: Eloi, Eloi, lama sabachthani'. He goes further and concludes the introduction with his longest and most moving account of the poet's condition:

> The ability to be in hell is a spiritual prerogative, and proclaims the true nature of such a being. Without darkness, in the world we know, the light would go unprized; without evil, goodness would have no meaning. Over every poet's door is nailed Keats's saying about negative capability. Poetry is born of the tensions set up by the poet's ability to be 'in uncertainties, mysteries, doubts, without any irritable reaching after fact and reason'. Without the section entitled 'Nothing' I feel that the contents of this anthology would have been incomplete and its poetry the poorer.

These are the insights that inform so much of *Pietà*. Though we have seen R. S. Thomas write movingly of the Nativity (albeit given an essentially 'manward' turn in its consideration of the culture of cities), of all those moments in which our faith is asserted in contemplation, the Crucifixion most securely holds his attention. The poem here, for which the collection is named, opens ambiguously:

> Always the same hills
> Crowd the horizon.

Where? In Wales or Israel? And the second stanza is deceptively simple, establishing an iconography which painting and the definitions of theology have examined with so much more diffuse a method:

> And in the foreground
> The tall Cross,
> Sombre, untenanted,
> Aches for the Body
> That is back in the cradle
> Of a maid's arms.

The conjunction of our more abstract terms, Crucifixion, Deposition, Pietà, conveys something of the poem's mystery, which paintings convey more concretely. Bellini, indeed, in two movingly associated paintings renders *The Virgin and Child* and the *Pietà* within almost identical landscapes, with the bodies of the Child and the Crucified precisely echoed in their posture, recumbent in the arms and lap of the Virgin. All this is contained, barely articulated, within this poem and with a remarkable additional attribution of longing to the Cross itself, an emotive image that reaches back to *The Dream of the Rood* in Old English:

> I trembled that the man clasped me, yet dared not bow,
> fall to the earth's corners, but I must stand fast.
> A Rood was I reared up, heaved up the strong King,
> Heaven's Lord; I dared not bend.
>
> (Trans. W.M.M.)

In 'Pietà', the Cross itself, seemingly insentient as it stands 'sombre, untenanted', yet actively and consciously 'aches for the Body' of the crucified Christ — metaphysical poetry in its sharpest conjunction.

This mood, in which dereliction is revealed as a creative spiritual force, has its powerful expression in 'Kierkegaard'. The progress of the imagery reads like a refashioning of the Passion narrative:

> . . .a warped
> Crucifix upon a hill
> In Jutland. . .
> . . .as though a bone
> Had broken in the adored body
> Of his God,

and as the dereliction closes upon Kierkegaard, his writings become, in an almost physical sense, his 'retreat':

> wounded, he crawled
> To the monastery of his chaste thought
> To offer up his crumpled amen.

This insight, in which the believer suffers a 'kenosis' analogous to that which is defined in St Paul's phrase, that Christ 'emptied himself, is familiar in R.S. Thomas's work and is the source and power of three fine poems in this volume. 'In Church', as so often, we are without any witness or congregation and its silent emptiness prompts the despairing question:

                    Is this where God hides
        From my searching?

But it is the setting for a quite different event, the desert-proving
of the solitary priest,

                    testing his faith
            On emptiness, nailing his questions
            One by one to an untenanted cross.

'The Belfry' is no home for carillons but stands 'gaunt',

                    terrible
            In its own way, for religion
            Is like that. There are times
            When a black frost is upon
            One's whole being, and the heart
            In its bone belfry hangs and is dumb.

Few have the endurance to penetrate far enough into the mystery
to reach this 'dark night of the soul' of which St John of the Cross
and the other mystics have taught us. Few, therefore, have the stead-
fastness of prayers which extend

            Steadily through the hard spell
            Of weather that is between God
            And himself. Perhaps they are warm rain
            That brings the sun and afterwards flowers
            On the raw graves and throbbing of bells.

It would be comforting to the reader's sense of orthodoxy if Thomas's
'dark night' were always to dawn in such proper surroundings as
a church or at least a belfry; in fact 'The Moor' becomes the setting
of the profoundest mystical experience:

            There were no prayers said. But stillness
            Of the heart's passions — that was praise
            Enough; and the mind's cession
            Of its kingdom. I walked on,
            Simple and poor, while the air crumbled
            And broke on me generously as bread.

This is not simply meditation, nor the elevation of mind into insight;
this is crowned in sacrament, in the breaking of bread.

                            55

IX

Here we may pause, to consider not wholly in sequence, two works which borrow a great deal of significance from each other, *The Mountains* (1968) and *Abercuawg* (1976). The former is a quite brief essay to accompany ten wood engravings by Reynolds Stone after drawings in Snowdonia by John Piper. The drawings have the atmospheric precision of an artist who had long made himself at home in the Snowdon range; the wood engravings have the cool accuracy of fine sculpture — like the carved lettering of which Reynolds Stone is a master. And R.S. Thomas's words have a corresponding precision, a sense of actual place. For Snowdonia is not primarily here a place to visit; it is a place for living:

> Further down the houses begin, the rows of drab dwellings wrenched from the slopes, with wet roofs, permanently wet. Their plots marked off with slate fences. Places of spittle and cold phlegm. Women swab the steps that are never dry. Late lonely buses climb up to them, a brief gaudiness in a vast gloom. These people know the mountains, but do not ascend them. They gnaw at them for small pay, and die early, silted up. The bare, hideous chapels ache for an hour with sad words and fierce singing; the futile memorials are planted in rows.

On the slopes themselves there is endeavour, sharp, even heroic, but

> It is not good to live by mountains. They demand human sacrifice. Every year somebody must die.

With this grim undertone it is difficult to convey, without reprinting the whole essay, the ultimate grace and charm of this writing. It centres upon its visionary quality, beyond the realities of biology and the hard economics of slate; in the final understanding of them, their mountains are

the summer pastures of the Celtic people...the high field green as
an emerald. This is the precious stone that a man sells all his goods
to possess.

And in a closing passage the tough facts of Snowdonia are
transmuted:

> It is to this that men return, in thought, in reality, seeking for something
> unnameable, a lost Eden, a lost childhood; for fulfilment, for escape,
> for refuge, for conquest of themselves, for peace, for adventure. The
> list is endless. The hills have all this to give and more.

To have understood slate quarries within a vision of Eden is to
have gone some little way towards *Abercuawg*. This remarkable
oration (his longest work in Welsh demands a title more evocative
than 'essay') was given at the National Eisteddfod in Cardigan in
1976. It is a delicately argued, convoluted work, redoubling upon
itself as it seeks to define the ideal and real identity of Llywarch Hen's
Abercuawg, 'that place where the cuckoos sing'. It is probably most
readily approached by way of the poem of the same title in his volume
Frequencies (1978). Here the quest is declared almost flatly:

> I am a seeker
> in time for that which is
> beyond time, that is everywhere
> and nowhere; no more before
> than after, yet always
> about to be; whose duration is
> of the mind, but free as
> Bergson would say of the mind's
> degradation of the eternal.

The mind is by no means the only agent of degradation. R. S. Thomas
gives us his most passionate attack here on the corruption of
'civilization':

> Ymha le bynnag y bo Abercuawg, y mae yno goed a chaeau a blodau
> a nentydd perloyw, dihalog, gyda'r cogau'n dal i ganu yno. Dros y fath
> le yr wyf yn barod i wneud aberth hyd angau efallai. Ond beth am
> le sydd rhy lawn o bobl, lle mae stryd ar ôl stryd o dai cyfoes, di-
> gymeriad, pob un a'i gwt modur a'i bolyn teledu; lle mae'r coed a'r
> adar a'r blodau wedi ffoi oddi arno o flaen cynnydd blynyddol y concrit

a'r macadam, lle mae'r bobl yn gwneud yr un math ar waith undonog a dienaid er mwyn cynnal mwy a mwy o'u tebyg?

(Wherever Abercuawg may be there we find trees and fields and flowers and clear, unpolluted streams, where the cuckoos still sing. For that kind of place I am willing to sacrifice, even, perhaps, to die. But what of a place too full of people, with street after street of characterless contemporary houses, each with its garage and television aerial; where the trees and the birds and the flowers have fled before the yearly invasion of concrete and macadam, where the people perform the same monotonous, soulless tasks in order to sustain more and more of their like fellows?)

It is difficult to do justice to the complexity of this work without extensive quotation. It ranges through linguistic, philosophic and social and political matters; a passage near the end probably best summarizes both its aim and manner:

Dyma ystâd dyn. Y mae ef bob amser ar fedr amgyffred Duw; ond yn gymaint â'i fod yn greadur ac yn feidrol, ni wna byth. 'Wêl ef byth mo Abercuawg ychwaith. Ond trwy geisio ei gweld, trwy hiraethu amdani, trwy wrthod derbyn ei bod yn perthyn i'r gorffennol, a'i bod wedi mynd i ebargofiant; trwy wrthod derbyn rhywbeth ail-law yn ei lle hi, fe lwydda i'w chadw hi fel posibilrwydd tragwyddol.

(This is man's condition. He is always about to comprehend God; but inasmuch as he is a creature and finite, he will never succeed. Nor will he ever see Abercuawg. But by trying to see it, by longing for it, by refusing to accept that it belongs to the past and has gone to oblivion; by refusing to accept something second-hand in its place, he will succeed in maintaining its eternal possibility.)

R. S. Thomas has never succeeded more eloquently in expressing the glory and the tragedy of the Welsh condition. It orchestrates all his moods, from the acrid to the grandly ideal and though he has rarely succeeded in his few attempts at Welsh poetry, this allusive, ambivalent and passionate work succeeds in a very noble rhetoric.

X

The most prolific decade in R. S. Thomas's writing is introduced by the puzzling, even confounding, volume, *Not That He Brought Flowers* (1968). This is a volume of antitheses, contradictions, even denials, and yet the antitheses meet in a dialectic that looks forward, four years later, to the volume *H'm*. Wales is set in apposition to Spain, belief to scepticism, the life of toil to that of sophistication, and there are equally powerful expressions of a sickness of spirit very near to dereliction and of a buoyant hope that looks forward to *Abercuawg*.

The poem 'Burgos' has been looked at earlier in this essay, the poem of

> sad priests, fingering
> Their beads, praying for the lost people
> Of the soil.

This elegiac lament for a land 'bitter with sage and thistle' changes its tone sharply when the subject is not Spain seen with objective compassion, but Wales felt along the blood. 'Reservoirs' is one of Thomas's most complex poems. It opens with a temperate rejection:

> There are places in Wales I don't go:
> Reservoirs that are the subconscious
> Of a people,

and it accelerates and changes to a metaphor of his own art:

> The serenity of their expression
> Revolts me, it is a pose
> For strangers, a watercolour's appeal
> To the mass, instead of the poem's
> Harsher conditions.

Time and again Thomas returns to this austere estimate of the poet's role, his commitment to prophecy, unmollifying and revealing. The second stanza opens with a tightening anger:

> Where can I go, then, from the smell
> Of decay, from the putrefying of a dead
> Nation?

and he moves from the hills of streams and reservoirs to the salt sea, traditional agent of cleansing and discovery:

> I have walked the shore
> For an hour and seen the English
> Scavenging among the remains
> Of our culture, covering the sand
> Like the tide and, with the roughness
> Of the tide, elbowing our language
> Into the grave that we have dug for it.

An 'objective reader' might suspect that this was a dubious emotion, a seeking for a scapegoat for a sin that lies elsewhere; he would be wrong on two counts: this is not an objective poem and its force of feeling drives towards no temperate logic; and at the same time there is a poised estimate — though the English may scavenge among the jetsam of a culture it is 'we' who have dug the grave. There are no facile resolutions in Thomas's later poems and we have to be prepared for an agility of argument which still allows scope for powerful emotion. Two themes, the life of the spirit and the austerity of the intellect, are brought into sharper focus in this collection than in any previous collection. The first is not argued but exemplified in 'St Julian and the Leper', a poem of great economy (of twelve short lines of verse). St Julian waits for the embrace of a leper, quietly ignoring danger and abhorrence,

> contaminating
> Himself with a kiss
> With the love that
> Our science has disinfected.

'Kneeling' has almost as great economy. We carry as its background the earlier poems of the expectant worshipper in an empty church, but the conclusion in this poem is profounder than simple revelation:

> Prompt me, God;
> But not yet. When I speak,
> Though it be you who speak
> Through me, something is lost.
> The meaning is in the waiting.

There is an ironic recollection — but to what a different end — of St Augustine in the words, 'But not yet ("Convert me, God, but not yet")', but the poem leads to no vision, no credal conclusion but simply to a process, a meditative patience, a 'waiting'. The allusions are manifold and obvious (the Psalmist's constant 'waiting still upon God', 'patiently tarrying' for the divine outcome, with the climax in the prophecy of Habakkuk, 'though the vision tarry, wait for it. . .it will be no time to linger'). There is no diminution, in these later volumes, of the passionate craving for truth, but rather a new maturity, a still patience and an awareness of 'occasion', of a divine amphitheatre:

> the sun's light
> Ringing me, as though I acted
> A great rôle,

and an awareness, as of the Epistle to the Hebrews, of the vast audience:

> all that close throng
> Of spirits waiting, as I
> For the message.

And there is the same new maturity and allusiveness in his exploration of the life of the intellect — 'After the Lecture'. In words and books he had found a climate

> That is rigorous though not too hard
> For the spirit,

and from this context he can move to the central dilemmas of the spiritual quest, where mind and aspiration meet in their search for the ineffable, 'one not to be penned in a concept',

> whose attributes are the negations
> Of thought, who holds us at bay with
> His symbols, the opposed emblems
> Of hawk and dove.

61

This exploration is an agonized searching *after* his lecture, when the intellect has had its way and stands aside for different insights and actions:

> What can my prayers win
> For the kindred souls brought to the bone
> To be tortured, and burning, burning
> Through history with their own strange light?

This is an astringent volume, with its own quiet triumphs but in which the sharpening insights, 'the shadow of the tree' falling 'On our acres like a crucifixion' ('That'), look forward to the still greater intensity of the next volume, *H'm*, for which we had to wait four years.

When, in 1972, it was published, we had the impression at first reading that this was the most organized, the most theologically orientated of the collections hitherto. Four credal themes appeared to dominate the volume: Creation, The Fall, Incarnation, Crucifixion; and in the complex interplay of these themes, a coherent pattern of thought appeared to emerge. But this was too comfortable an assumption; a very central poem, 'Via Negativa', closely links this book to *Not That He Brought Flowers*. The purely intellectual assumptions are familiar enough:

> (God) keeps the interstices
> In our knowledge, the darkness
> Between the stars.

But the fullest expression of this negative knowledge takes us back to the 'waiting' of the earlier volume:

> God is that great absence
> In our lives, the empty silence
> Within, the place where we go
> Seeking, not in hope to
> Arrive or find,

and if, like St Thomas, we seek palpable assurance,

> We put our hands in
> His side hoping to find
> It warm

and are denied the comfort. In 'Petition', earlier in the book, he had warned us of this outcome:

> One thing I have asked
> Of the disposer of the issues
> Of life: that truth should defer
> To beauty. It was not granted.

What then of the major issues in his structure of belief? They are clearly there and in an abstract criticism could be distinguished and isolated. But they are not the expression of an intellectual and formal abstraction; to treat of Creation before 'the flaw took over' ('Soliloquy'), of Crucifixion without realizing the agony within the Incarnation, is to falsify R. S. Thomas's work in this volume. The latter instance is powerfully and movingly exemplified in 'The Coming'. There is conversation in eternity, God showing the son a small globe, with 'a scorched land of fierce colour'. At its centre a simple object:

> On a bare
> Hill a bare tree saddened
> The sky. Many people
> Held out their thin arms
> To it.

They expect an April, that cruellest month and the month of the Resurrection; the son responds:

> Let me go there, he said.

Creation is an ambiguous art. 'Once' has undertones both of Genesis and *Paradise Lost*. Man emerges before the greater part of the material order and, like a Moses or Elijah, hides in fear 'in the side of the mountain'. Woman joins him, 'out of the depths of myself', and, like Milton's Adam and Eve at the expulsion from Eden:

> I took your hand,
> Remembering you, and together,
> Confederates of the natural day,
> We went forth to meet the Machine.

Creation almost subsumes the Fall and it in turn looks to its fruit, man's mechanistic ingenuity. There are moments indeed when

Creation is almost an act of cruelty. 'Echoes' relates a troubled emergence of singing creatures and hands 'curious to build'. And the closing words are like an affront:

> On the altars
> They made him the red blood
> Told what he wished to hear,

an affront that is reduplicated in 'The Island':

> And their women shall bring forth
> On my altars, and I will choose the best
> Of them to be thrown back into the sea.

But this tone is adjusted to the harmony of 'Making', a quietly 'evolutionary' account of creation leading to 'an absence' which God found ·disturbing:

> I slept and dreamed
> Of a likeness, fashioning it,
> When I woke, to a slow
> Music; in love with it
> For itself, giving it freedom
> To love me; risking the disappointment,

a poem remarkably successful technically, in the fullness of its end-stopped statements, which at the same time prepare for a new development in the turn of the lines.

The fullest — and the simplest — statement of R.S. Thomas's brooding on the Incarnation comes in the very brief lyric, 'Song'. There is a childlike evocation of folklore — 'white', 'red', 'Holly berries' — and the Robin, which,

> like Christ
> Comes to us in his weakness,
> But with a sharp song,

another instance of the momentary irony which touches so many closing lines in his poetry.

Crucifixion is 'the green tree / Where history nailed him', and this history goes back a long way. The struggle between Cain and Abel, a struggle not simply of wounds but of modes of sacrifice ('Cain'), issues in the insight that in this conflict the Trinity is itself engaged:

> I anointed myself
> In readiness for the journey
> To the doomed tree you were at work upon,

an engagement which is constant and recurring through the work
of poets, theologians and scientists ('Repeat'), as God

> returned
> To his centre to await their coming for him.
> It was not his first time to be crucified.

The machine sounds throughout the collection, marking the nadir
of our civilization; it even plays its part in crucifixion — though
without the redemption that issues from it:

> The machine replaces
> The hand that fastened you
> To the cross, but cannot absolve us.
> ('Earth')

'No Answer', 'Digest', 'Postscript', all make their varied attack on the
machine culture which crushes 'the creeds and masterpieces' and
still proposes 'no answers'.

There are echoes here of other, earlier and perhaps remote worlds
of reference (of Job and Aeschylus, Yeats and Ben Shahn) but the
central tension by which this volume lives is found in the relation
between two poems, 'H'm' and 'The Kingdom' which occupy
successive pages. The former (its speaking-tone distinct as a Chinese
ideogram or the inflexion of R.S. Thomas's voice) seems convention-
ally to relate the preacher to his God, words trying and failing and
a gesture attempting speech:

> reaching
> his arms out but the little
> children the ones with
> big bellies and bow
> legs that were like
> a razor shell
> were too weak to come.

This is the most pungent statement in this collection of the 'problem'
which echoes throughout it, of the incomprehensible results of 'the

flaw', that aberration at the heart of things. R. S. Thomas makes no more attempt than this to articulate the tragedy; certainly no more than any honest theologian does he attempt a resolution. Quite simply he places alongside it, without irony and without argument, the other intuition which runs counter. 'The Kingdom' is 'a long way off' but does not ignore the poor man, the consumptive, the blind,

> The bent bones and the minds fractured
> By life.

Remote the Kingdom may be,

> but to get
> There takes no time and admission
> Is free, if you will purge yourself
> Of desire, and present yourself with
> Your need only and the simple offering
> Of your faith, green as a leaf.

There is a rare tone in Thomas's voice; all the more remarkable that it comes in this most mature, most acrid and clear-sighted collection of poems.

What is a Welshman? (1974) is an unhappy little volume of a dozen poems, of which the wry titles are frequently the best part ('He lies down to be counted, On a diet of warmed-up music'); many of them are too content to rewrite former postures:

> In Wales there are
> no crocodiles, but the tears
> continue to flow from
> their slimed sources...
> Anything to
> sell? cries the tourist
> to the native rummaging among
> the remnants of his self-respect,

and there is an over-facile parody in the political satire of 'He has the vote':

> VOTE PLAID, mun
> and be damned for your own sake.

66

But in its quick anger and conversational tone it rids the poet of attitudes which find no place in the collection, *Laboratories of the Spirit*, which appeared in the following year. This is a book at once bleak and exhilarating, like traversing a high col. The vocabulary has substantially changed, raiding a hitherto alien world: 'the crucible of the adult mind, the tall city of glass that is the laboratory of the spirit, the mind's stare into the lenses' furious interiors'. Even the conditions and context of the poet's struggle have shifted; for 'our nightmares are intellectual'. There is a firm acceptance in these poems of facts and attitudes which were formerly matters of rebellion; indeed the first poem ('Emerging') sets the key:

> Not as in the old days I pray
> God. My life is not what it was.
> Yours, too, accepts the presence of
> the machine?

and there is a consciously new maturity:

> the emerging
> from the adolescence of nature
> into the adult geometry
> of the mind.

These same terms are now accepted as the conditions for a certain vision of God:

> see my beauty
> in the angles between
> stars, in the equations
> of my kingdom.
> ('Mediations')

With a change to another science, even the mystical 'dark night' is restated:

> The darkness
> is the deepening shadow
> of your presence; the silence a
> process in the metabolism
> of the being of love,

and all this shaping its meaning within 'the sleepless conurbations of the stars' ('Alive'). With this change in vocabulary a great deal of his angry expression of anguish has been muted. It is true that the poet's compulsion to 'write what it is to be man' issues in the single word 'lonely' and in his vision of 'The Bright Field' in which the treasure is hidden, he has to renounce all he has to possess it; but this is declared with a new serenity, no longer a hankering for 'a receding future' or 'an imagined past' but in a more tranquil activity:

> It is the turning
> aside like Moses to the miracle
> of the lit bush, to a brightness
> that seemed as transitory as your youth
> once, but is the eternity that awaits you.

The Crucifixion still looms over all the theological insights and with none of the tragic paradoxes avoided — 'God needs his martyrdom' ('Amen'), but the former agony of the empty prayer is now resolved and with a new vision of the Cross:

> Deliver me from the long drought
> of the mind, Let leaves
> from the deciduous Cross
> fall on us, washing
> us clean, turning our autumn
> to gold by the affluence of their fountain.
> ('The Prayer')

Wales is a more tranquil (and rarer) presence in this volume, felt in the stillness of Llŷn and the gentle vision of Ann Griffiths; but the outer world of art is invoked more freely — Degas, Veneziano, Yeats and Athens, Karamazov and Ming, and (in 'Taste') a satirical conspectus of English literature in rhymed couplets ('amoeba...vers libre') with its gentle warning to such essays as this, against the 'critics' compulsive hurry to place a poet'.

This assured tone extends through all the themes and finally turns back upon R. S. Thomas himself, in the rueful, ironic, self-cauterizing 'Self-Portrait':

> All that skill,
> life, on the carving
> of the curved nostril and to no end

but disgust. The hurrying eyes
pause, waiting for an outdistanced
gladness to overtake them.

It is proper, however, to remember that the volume that contained
this insight also speaks of 'the serenity of art'.

Two years later, in 1977, appeared the little volume of eighteen
poems, *The Way of It*, published by the Ceolfrith Press, with drawings
by Barry Hirst. This forms a most interesting bridge between
Laboratories of the Spirit and his next volume, *Frequencies*; indeed it
is difficult to deny one's feeling that these are three 'movements' in
one large-scale work, in which old themes are transmuted and new
themes given powerful expression.

Theology here begins to be concerned with language and the
articulation of the inexpressible. There is a new definition of what
hitherto R.S. Thomas had simply called the silence of God; for God
has ways of speech beyond words:

> Whose silence so eloquent
> as his? What word so explosive
> as that one Palestinian
> word with the endlessness of its fall-out?
> ('Nuclear')

and this is extended with a new clarity in the poem, 'Praise', in which
God mobilizes, for communication with man, the skills and
vocabulary of artist and scientist:

> When I am somewhat
> fearful of your power,
> your ability to work miracles
> with a set-square, I hear
> you murmuring to yourself
> in a notation Beethoven
> dreamed of but never achieved.

But this divine virtuosity has another aspect:

> You speak
> all languages and none,
> answering our most complex
> prayers with the simplicity
> of a flower.

Man's responses in this little volume are not confined to the divine; there is a sharpened awareness of the supreme validity and therefore the tragic failures of human relationships. Ruefully the poet realizes within marriage that,

> if there are thorns
> in my life, it is she who
> will press her breast to them and sing,
> ('The Way of It')

and, more tragically, since related to a wider context, there is the realization of what constitutes 'the true human pain':

> It is the memories
> that one has, the impenitent bungler
> of love, refusing for too long
> to say 'yes' to that earlier gesture
> of love that had brought one
> forth.

This unpretentious little volume is the gathering of tone and gesture for the next — and for many of us the greatest — volume of R. S. Thomas's poetry, *Frequencies* (1978). It is his largest collection for many years and the most monumental. The themes are few (their lines established in *Laboratories of the Spirit*) and handled with an assured restraint, the least obtrusive being his return to the matter of Wales. Two poems, 'The Small Country' and 'Gone?', make clear affirmations; the first, that everything

> on this shrinking planet favours the survival
> of the small people, whose horizons
> are large only because they are content to look at them
> from their own hills.

The second poem returns to 'Prytherch country', now perhaps disappearing, but maintaining the assured acceptance of a man

> who has needs in him that only
> bare ground, black thorns and the sky's
> emptiness can fulfil.

The demands and the expectations are modest and limited but they still constitute for the poet the inescapable context of his vision.

But there is now a wider and deeper concern, pursued with all the old astringency but accepting with tranquillity the consequences of his exploration. The topic explored is nothing less than 'The Gap' between God and our articulations of his being:

> that is the grammarian's
> torment and the mystery
> at the cell's core, and the equation
> that will not come out, and is
> the narrowness that we stare
> over into the eternal
> silence that is the repose of God.

More than half the poems in this volume are variations on this theme, a collective driving-force felt in no earlier book of Thomas's. Philosophy can provide him with few definitions and indeed in one poem, 'Synopsis', he eschews the intellectual modes of all philosophers from Plato to Kierkegaard; for this exploration enters the 'infinite darkness between points of light'; seeking a vantage-point, of necessity he can find none:

> Face to face? Ah, no
> God; such language falsifies
> the relation. Nor side by side
> nor near you, nor anywhere
> in time and space.

In this absence of a known territory he must now trust himself, poised over 'an immense depth', to waiting,

> somewhere between faith and doubt.

For R.S. Thomas, speaking in his own person, this is the only language, the language of negatives explored by the mystics; since

> Godhead
> is the colonisation by mind
> of untenanted space,

it is without precedent, wholly self-subsistent, 'its own light', and if definition is attempted it is found to be

a statement beyond language
of conceptual truth.

The only person he finds through whom to speak is, characteristically,
Roger Bacon, who ventured daringly into strange knowledge, yet
came in the end to a conclusion beyond knowledge:

> He dreamed on in curves
>   and equations
> with the smell of saltpetre
> in his nostrils, and saw the hole
>   in God's side that is the wound
>   of knowledge and
> thrust his hand in it and believed.

And there is a metaphor that operates with truth and reconciles
the agonized search with the commonplace and the mundane:

> As form in sculpture is the prisoner
> of the hard rock, so in everyday life
> it is the plain facts and natural happenings
> that conceal God and reveal him to us
> little by little under the mind's tooling.

It is a disciplined and humble conclusion reached by a poetic
intelligence of rare honesty and astringency; which has passed
through many moods, pitying, defiant, compassionate and yet full
of disgust, with an idealism that permits itself no evasion, no lie;
which has posed for itself the noblest problems, of race, of vocation,
of 'exploration into God'. It is fitting that the closing lines of this
volume should constitute a kind of coda to the fourteen collections
of poetry that preceded it and should appear to summarize their
aspiration:

> Was the pilgrimage
> I made to come to my own
> self, to learn that in times
> like these and for one like me
> God will never be plain and
> out there, but dark rather and
> inexplicable, as though he were in here?

72

Criticism of the poetry of R.S. Thomas has never, over the past quarter century, been easy; to an unusual degree it has inevitably led from the poems to a personal evaluation of the poet, and, even more dangerous terrain, of the 'poet as priest'. It is then not surprising that one of the acutest comments on his work should have spilled over into wider implications; Harri Webb wrote in the R.S. Thomas number of *Poetry Wales* (Spring 1972):

> We have been fortunate to have two great and dissimilar poets to extend the frontiers of our land in different directions. Dylan gave us a country in which it was lovely to be a child, his successor as *Prifardd* of English-speaking Wales has given us a country in which it is necessary to be a man. I don't think we could ask for better guidance.

A Selected Bibliography

R. S. THOMAS

The Poetry:
The Stones of the Field (Druid Press, 1946).
An Acre of Land (Montgomeryshire Printing Company, 1952).
The Minister (Montgomeryshire Printing Company, 1953).
Song at the Year's Turning: Poems 1942-1954 (Rupert Hart-Davis, 1955).
Poetry for Supper (Rupert Hart-Davis, 1958).
Judgment Day, with drawings by Ceri Richards (Poetry Book Society, 1960).
Tares (Rupert Hart-Davis, 1961).
The Bread of Truth (Rupert Hart-Davis, 1963).
Pietà (Rupert Hart-Davis, 1966).
Not That He Brought Flowers (Rupert Hart-Davis, 1968).
Postcard: Song (Fishpaste Postcard Series, 1968).
The Mountains, with wood-engravings by Reynolds Stone after drawings by John Piper (Chilmark Press, 1968).
H'm (Macmillan, 1972).
Young and Old (Chatto and Windus, 1972).
Selected Poems 1946–1968 (Hart-Davis Macgibbon, 1973).
What is a Welshman? (Christopher Davies, 1974).
Laboratories of the Spirit (Macmillan, 1975).
The Way of It, with drawings by Barry Hirst (Ceolfrith Press, 1977).
Frequencies (Macmillan, 1978).
Between Here and Now (Macmillan, 1981).
Destinations (The Celandine Press, 1985).
Ingrowing Thoughts (Poetry Wales Press, 1985).
Experimenting with an Amen (Macmillan, 1986).
Experimenting with an Amen (Papermac, 1988).

The Echoes Return Slow (Macmillan, 1988).
Later Poems, A Selection (Macmillan, 1981).

Prose Works:
R.S. Thomas contributed frequently to Wales, Y Fflam and Y Faner
and there is an important survey of his 'Occasional Prose' by Randal
Jenkins in the 'R.S. Thomas Number' of Poetry Wales (Spring 1972,
Vol. 7, No. 4, edited by Meic Stephens). Three longer prose works
merit special entries:

Words and the Poet, W. D. Thomas Memorial Lecture (University of
Wales Press, 1964).
Abercuawg, Y ddarlith lenyddol flynyddol, Eisteddfod Genedlaethol
Cymru Aberteifi a'r Cylch, Gwasg Gomer, 1976 — National
Eisteddfod Annual Literary Lecture, Cardigan (Gomer Press, 1976).
'The Creative Writer's Suicide', Planet 41 (January 1978), a lecture
delivered at the 1977 Annual Rally of the Department of Extra-Mural
Studies, University College of Wales, Aberystwyth. The Welsh
original 'Hunan-Laddiad Y Llenor' published in Taliesin, December
1977.
R. S. Thomas, Selected Prose, edited by Sandra Anstey (Bridgend, 1983).
Selected Prose, R.S. Thomas, edited by Sandra Anstey (Bridgend, 1986).

Anthologies edited by R.S. Thomas:
The Batsford Book of Country Verse (Batsford, 1961).
The Penguin Book of Religious Verse (Penguin, 1963).
Edward Thomas: Selected Poems (Faber, 1964).
A Choice of George Herbert's Verse (Faber, 1967).
A Choice of Wordsworth's Verse (Faber, 1971).

Broadcasts:
The Minister was first written for broadcasting by the BBC (Cardiff),
18 September 1952.

A transcript of John Ormond's film for BBC Television (2 April 1972),
'R.S. Thomas: Priest And Poet', was published with an introduction
by Sam Adams in the 'R.S. Thomas Number' of Poetry Wales (Spring
1972).

The radio broadcast 'Y Llwybrau Gynt' (Early Recollections) was published in the second volume of that title, edited by Alun Oldfield-Davies (Gwasg Gomer, 1972).

A stereo recording, 'R. S. Thomas reading his own poems', was issued by the Welsh Arts Council, in Oriel Records, in 1976.

Selected Criticism:

W.M. Merchant, 'Since 1950: R. S. Thomas', in the *Critical Quarterly*, II, 4, 1960.

R. G. Thomas, 'The Poetry of R. S. Thomas', in *A Review Of English Literature*, III, 4, 1962.

R. George Thomas, *Writers And Their Works (No. 166): R. S. Thomas* (Longmans for the British Council, 1964).

M. Stephens (ed.), *Poetry Wales*, a special R. S. Thomas number, 7, 4, Spring 1972; critical essays by John Ackerman, Roland Mathias, Dafydd Elis Thomas, Anthony Conran, Sam Adams, R. George Thomas and Jeremy Hooker, with the review of R. S. Thomas's prose works by Randal Jenkins noted above and a 'letter' by Harri Webb quoted above in this essay.

C. Obedient, Essay on R. S. Thomas, in *Eight Contemporary Poets* (Oxford University Press, 1974).

A. E. Dyson, 'The Poetry of R. S. Thomas', *Critical Quarterly* XX, 2, Summer 1978.

The Author

Moelwyn Merchant was born in Port Talbot in 1913 and graduated at University College, Cardiff, where he returned in 1940 as a lecturer in English. He graduated D.Litt. in 1959 and was appointed Reader in English Literature in the University of Wales in 1960; in the same year he became Professor of English at the University of Exeter. He is an honorary Canon of Salisbury, having been Chancellor of the Cathedral for five years. He has been a Fellow of the Folger Library, Washington DC, Willett Professor in the University of Chicago, is an honorary graduate of the University of Wittenberg, Ohio, and a Fellow of the Royal Society of Literature. In 1974 he became Vicar of Llanddewibrefi in Dyfed, directed the Llanddewibrefi Festival of the Arts and was an honorary Fellow of the University College of Wales, Aberystwyth. He now lives in retirement in Leamington Spa.

His publications include the Reynard *Wordsworth* (Rupert Hart-Davis, 1955), *Shakespeare and the Artist* (Oxford University Press, 1959), *Creed and Drama* (SPCK, 1965), *Comedy* (Methuen, 1972), the Penguin edition of *The Merchant Of Venice* (1967), *No Dark Glass* (Christopher Davies, 1979), *Confrontation of Angels* (Christopher Davies, 1986), and two novels, *Jeshua* (Christopher Davies, 1987) and *Fire from the Heights* (Christopher Davies, 1988). He has had some thirty exhibitions of his sculpture.